HENRY BOUCHA:
STAR OF THE NORTH

HENRY BOUCHA:
STAR OF THE NORTH

MARY HALVERSON SCHOFIELD

Snowshoe Press

This is a biographical sketch.

Library of Congress No. 99-97237

For information, please address:

Snowshoe Press
P.O. Box 24334
Edina, MN 55424

Printed in the United States of America by M and M Printing, Inc., Minneapolis

Front cover photo: MINNEAPOLIS STAR TRIBUNE/Minneapolis-St. Paul
Back cover photo: BRUCE BENNETT STUDIOS

EDITED BY
COLLEEN WASNER AND DAVID STARKE

In memory of Alice and George Boucha

TABLE OF CONTENTS

FOREWORD

There are hundreds of books on big-name athletes who achieved fame and fortune and shared their stories of glory in books. Mary Schofield's work, however, goes beyond that in her entertaining and enlightening book that focuses on Minnesota's mystical sports hero and his ascent to the top in the world of hockey -- only to be ended by a brutal act of a hockey "goon."

This is the story of a Native American super-athlete: his humble beginnings in a remote log cabin on an Indian reserve; his rise to state adulation; his Olympic glory; and his brief fling at stardom in the National Hockey League. The book is a very intriguing one and will evoke emotions from anyone who reads it.

Murray Williamson, All-American
Coach of the 1972 Silver Olympians

Every now and then, since the dawning of mankind, one exceptional human will push the cover up and rise above the masses. When this happens, humanity takes note and recognizes that individual as above and apart...separate from the ordinary. We label these phenomena great: we learn their names. They belong to us in a collective way to hold high, to take pride in what they have achieved and to believe that they are connected to us in the spiritual bond of what is possible to attain on this earth when one stretches the bounds.

This story is about one of these elite. Born in the wild upper reaches of Minnesota of humble Ojibway-French roots, self-driven to be the best, and a legend by seventeen: Henry Boucha was master of the ice. He was a fiery champion for a ten-year span -- who could have continued reaching new heights for years to come -- but, instead, was brutally struck down by the barbaric act of another kind of human.

This book captures the bright years of the star who made his audiences hold their breath, who gave them goose-bumps and a dream that lifted them out of their doldrums, and who set their hearts flying with him across the ice sheets that were his kingdom.

***

...Mary Halverson Schofield

PROLOGUE

The first time I heard the name Henry Boucha was from friends, Pat and Betsy Houlihan. I had met this wonderful couple while I was attending Wisconsin State, Oshkosh, in the fall of 1969. They had immigrated to the mid-west from Connecticut. Pat had recently earned his Master's from the University of Minnesota and was now on the next step of his career, teaching anthropology before going on for his Ph.D. He and Betsy had lived in Minneapolis through the early months of 1969.

Over a dinner party I attended at their home, which included other college teaching staff, the conversation turned to the Houlihans talking, animatedly, about an amazing Indian-boy high school hockey player from Warroad, Minnesota. They were absolutely on fire about this kid, captivating their listeners as they spoke about him. "You've never seen anything like it," they reported, "It was so exciting," they went on. "The whole thing *hit* us so, we were staggered," they bubbled. "It was all anyone was talking about: the boy held the whole state hostage!" "We were glued to our tvs when his games were on."

Henry Boucha had made an impact on these scholarly people. I remembered, at the time, thinking how odd this was: sitting around a candlelit table, with intellectuals from different areas of the country, conversing excitedly about something as obscure as Minnesota high school hockey -- and a youngster from an out-of-the-way, pint-sized town, who had the ability to affect, evidently, all walks of life.

***

My first trip to Warroad, to interview its legendary Henry Boucha, gave me a preview of the hearted roots he came from. As I waited, in the dead of winter, at Signature Airways across the runway from the Minneapolis – St. Paul terminal, to board a Marvin Windows twelve-seat plane that would take me to the north rim of Minnesota, a humble, unassuming, slightly built gentleman, carrying only a plastic bag, came quietly into the well-appointed, softly colored lobby and took a seat across from me. The receptionist set out cookies and coffee and said we would board soon.

I asked the man if he had flown to Warroad before. He spoke to me through a throat microphone that monotoned he had come for cancer treatment. He said he was in pain. His name was Harf and he was from Greenbush, which was west of Warroad, and he flew down from Warroad to the V.A. hospital for treatments often. The Marvins, who owned the window company, and the airplane, he said, did not charge him for the flights. Flights of mercy, I thought. The Marvins of the window company have a soul.

Several businessmen, chatting loudly, hurriedly entered the mini-terminal and the pilot, who was waiting for them, signaled for us to board. The men, who had business with Marvin Windows, rushed out to the plane. I started to pick up my luggage but the very ill man wrestled me out of the largest one with surprising strength and insisted he carry it. As we walked the tarmac through the hard winter wind to board the tiny plane, I thought of the kindly man who walked, bent over, carrying my suitcase with a stubborn built-in chivalry, and how caring for someone else was of primary importance to him. I wondered what I would find at the end of the flight in this town called Warroad.

The pilot hoisted the baggage into the hollow tail, which was part of the inside of the plane, as we boarded. Harf and I were the last to board, unnoticed by the men heading to business in the North country.

After takeoff the folksy pilot asked us all if wanted coffee out of a thermos he had carried on board, then he settled down to read a paper for the duration of the flight. The clouds huddled between the plane and the ground, covering Minnesota for the duration of the flight. Harf and I chatted some and I browsed a book on Minnesota bogs. I thought about my long-time friendship with the Houlihans and the many years since I had first heard about Henry from them. Then, as we slanted for the landing, I could see Lake of the Woods off to the Northeast. The sun was orange and dipping in the west, but gave enough of a glow for us to see the sprawling snow-coated lake. The bitter wind struck us again as we disembarked. I said my goodbyes to Harf. Henry Boucha, the legend, was there to meet me.

I had met Henry previously but was struck again by his height, his quiet dominating presence and soft, sincere eyes. Now I would also meet the people from Warroad who had encouraged him as a child, cheered for him as a youth, and stood paralyzed when the fates abandoned him.

For two days I toured the pristine little town and spoke with its residents. I was acutely aware of their warmth and genuineness. The ice rink ranks in the top I have ever seen; the library and Heritage Center, the loveliest. Ruth Stukel, of the Heritage Center, had materials ready for me. The schools were impressive: one is first struck with how clean they are and next delighted with the beautiful artwork throughout...from the mural in the high school to the children's creations in the grade school. A back-to-basics attitude was there and the children looked honestly happy. I saw a volunteer sitting in the hall with a child who was reading out loud to her. As a teacher I had the sense that education is handleable in Warroad and its children are not falling through the cracks. Warroad's residents had a state of the art indoor swimming pool. The Marvins had a lot to do with the amenities of this bustling town and, though I did not meet them, I could feel them and their sense of community everywhere we went.

Henry drove us by the Christian Hockey Stick factory, owned by 1960 Olympic hockey stars, Roger and Billy Christian. We saw where the old Booth fish factory had been on the shores of the Warroad River and we looked across to Government Island where Henry and other Warroad boys had skated as children. We stopped at the city park to look over the winter-dead Lake of the Woods with Arctic Cat using its surface for testing snowmobiles.

During our visit to the ice rink Henry turned on the bright lights. Dull lights were burning already and I could make out something moving on the ice surface while we were waiting for the bright lights to warm up. When the lights blinked on we saw a small boy, about four years old, scooting across the ice toward his father at what, I am sure, was record speed for a tot. He couldn't stop without sitting, splatting into the boards or falling...all of which he did enthusiastically, uttering no complaints. His last effort was a bonsai run for the door, falling out onto the rubber matting outside the rink. When he got his breath he smiled brightly and yelled, "I'm getting better, Dad!" As I stood there next to Warroad's most famous son, I was struck with the fact that Henry cared about this little boy; this new generation that would step up to take his place.

My intrigue with Warroad, its superstar, and its people who, though modern, hail from another time...a gracious time...a time I had known many years before, had begun.

1

For the love of Henry

The screaming 15,000 fans in the brightly lit Met Center rose to their feet in one immense swell as the scrappy Warroad Warriors hockey team, from the tiny town so far north it almost touched Canada, skated onto the ice for the 1969 Minnesota State High School Championship. Their entrance sent a charge through the crowd like an invisible bolt of lightning, causing the fans to cheer, yell, whistle and clap in unbridled ecstasy. The ovation lasted five full minutes as the teenage boys, trying to act nonchalant but feeling numb knots in their stomachs, tried to absorb its meaning.

Warroad's Coach Roberts, knowing full well the meaning of this tribute, stood looking up at the tumultuous fans emotionally. He had hardly had time to reflect on these last few weeks and now surely wasn't the time, but he felt the sense of history being made. His team had worked miracles to get here and they deserved this rip-roaring homage.

Waroad's team was captained by #16, the legendary seventeen-year-old American Indian boy, Henry Boucha. Henry had led this underdog team "seat of their pants" style to this final game of the 1969 Minnesota State High School Championship.

Again, as he had many times over the years, Roberts asked himself how he could have been lucky enough to have coached this phenomenal kid, this poised and mystical figure, whom he was convinced was the finest hockey player to have ever come out of Minnesota.

One small section of the arena held the "green jackets," possibly a thousand strong: the rival Edina supporters from the wealthy suburban school, who had been labeled "cake eaters" by the less monied. The rest of the fans were cheering for the underdog team from little Warroad, the Cinderella team of the tournament.

Lanky Henry Boucha stepped onto the glimmering ice almost lazily. He skated slowly around the large frozen oval toying with a puck as the other skaters whizzed by him. He was six feet tall and looked mostly arms and legs. His hockey breezers were too short, as was his ill-fitting jersey, and he looked out of place among the other skaters. Henry had an uncanny sense of peace about him as he stretched and shook out his shoulders. He didn't seem to notice the other players or, for that matter, the insane crowd that was cheering, for the most part, for him. Henry looked, for all the world, like a lollygagger: someone to watch from the bench and possibly give the other skaters encouragement.

The crowd knew better. They quieted as the warm-ups started but kept their gaze on Henry because they knew that when the spirit moved him Henry would put on his show. He casually skated around the far end, coming from behind the net, and almost seemed to yawn as he started down ice. The crowd readied expectantly as they saw a patch of clear ice open up as the players ahead of him rounded the net on the other end. Henry twitched slightly and then, as if he had been ignited like a Roman candle, his bulk streaked down the ice. The sight was electrifying and the delighted crowd exuded an admiring, prolonged *ooooooooooooooooooohhhhhhhhhhhhhhh.*

Glen Carlson, a former Minnesota All-Stater from the '56 Thief River Falls state championship hockey team, was watching from good seats at the blue line on the south side of the Met Center. "Damdest thing I've ever seen in my life," he said to his friend. The friend nodded as he kept an intent eye on Henry.

Henry settled back into his slow and quiet routine as the crowd marveled and waited expectantly for another burst. They were not to be disappointed. Henry let his teammates get ahead of him again and then he took off pounding like a startled deer as he skimmed the ice. The crowd *oooooooooooohhhhhhhhhed* again; this time he didn't pause in between sprints but kept it going like a double axle. *Swoosh,* like a bat out of hell, he tore up the ice, thrilling the spectators again and this time they *oooooooooooohhhhhhhhhhhhhhhhhhhed* even longer.

The current in the air held a silent whisper that told the fans before hand that this game would thereafter be known as the game of games of any Minnesota State High School Tournament championship contest. The Minneapolis newspapers hailed it as a David and Goliath event. Could the team from the raw edges of the north with its superstar #16 beat the powerhouse team from the large and privileged school?

Cameras flashed and tvs strained to keep up with Henry. The media couldn't get enough of him. He was a sensation, "the rage," and everyone wanted a piece of his action.

The teams gathered for their introductions, which hushed the crowd in preparation of the announcements of the boys' names. The Edina team was introduced first to a few "yea, rah rah's" as each player skated out to center ice as his name was called. The crowd had a 'lets get on with it' attitude as they waited. Then the charge ignited again as the booming voice said, "And now for the Warroad Warriors!" As each Warrior shot out to center ice, a rousing cheer went up from the stands. The announcer skipped #16 and then, after the entire Warroad team had been announced, he took a deep breath and, like an ancient announcing the Roman Emperor, he almost sang: "Hen-er-y Booooou-chaaaa!" Henry skated out low and long to the thunderous ovation...dazzling the standing, screaming mob whose applause gave him butterflies in his stomach. They did not let up their boisterous salute to him for a full ten minutes.

The fans envisioned this Indian boy from the north living in a teepee and eating wild rice when he wasn't amazing them on the ice. He was a pure hero of heroes, who spoke to their hearts. There was no doubt about it; the fans loved Henry Boucha.

PART I

EARLY CHILDHOOD

MIJAKWAD... "IT IS FINE, CLEAR WITH SUNSHINE"
OJIBWAY

2

Ojibway

The rosy shadows of early morning flung themselves across the snow that lay like risen cream on the thickly frozen lake. The winds had pushed the snow into wave-like formations, and the cold froze them there, giving the eerie effect of a motionless pastel ocean.

Bundled-up three-year-old Henry galloped across the lake-scape, jumping the small jutting ridges. The wind stung his face and tears froze on his cheeks, but he was happy: he was going to see his father. His mother was walking behind him, carrying his younger brother, Eddie.

The cold and wind didn't matter to Henry because all that was on the mind of the child was seeing his father, and his eyes squinted across the snow for the first glimpse. In the distance he saw the men. He couldn't hear them yet, but he knew they would be sawing the ice, or pulling in the nets of slippery cold fish that they sold to the Booth or Selvog fish companies.

In the summer, Henry's father took his wooden fishing boat on the lake and cast his nets into the open waters, but in the fall his father dragged the boat out of the water on rollers onto the beach at Warroad. In the winter, the men, commercial fisherman, worked on the frigid ice, bracing themselves against the sub-zero temperatures and whipping winds to earn a living for their families.

Henry was Ojibway, from the nation of Hiawatha. His roots streaked back across generations of North American Indians. His great-grandmother, Maymushagubiek, Laughing Mary, a medicine woman, was a healer of her people.

Henry's mother spoke Ojibway with her birth family but the mysterious language died with her; it was not fashionable to speak her native tongue and she did not pass it onto her children. The light-skinned men who conquered the North American continent believed in the "survival of the fittest" and justified their deplorable actions by insisting that the American Indian was not the fittest because he did not have gunpowder and could not win the battles against the newcomers. These intruders to the Indian lands, who had broken one hundred and sixty-one treaties with the native peoples, were continuing to break the Indian spirit and culture.

The mid-1950's, when Henry was a child, was a time when being born an American Indian was to be born with shame.

Native roots were being pulled out, ancient traditional religion was ridiculed and white man's philosophy was being foisted on them as the "only way." Peoples who had inhabited a land for thousands of years teetered towards their genocidal end. Some would think, when the boy grew up, that all traces of his ancestry and tradition would have been wiped out, but for now, as the boy's little body sprinted toward his father, he was not aware of the catastrophe that surrounded his people. He was also unaware that the die had been cast within him. The Indian tradition would not stop with the boy's mother. Ojibway drums that were not to be quieted would beat in his soul and Ojibway roots of a millennium were even now twining quietly within the boy. He was an extension of a people who had a spiritual connection to nature. He was melded to a people of daring and courage. He was part of a people who lived in harmony with the Earth, who were waiting for the prophecy of the old medicine man for the "Eagle to Land on the Moon" so Indian people could rise again. The child was Henry Boucha and he was running across a part of the expansive Lake of the Woods where his forefathers had lived for centuries.

Little Henry raced up to his father, but his father was busy pulling in the nets from the openings the men had hand sawed through the ice. Henry watched as his father and the men sorted the fish carefully and tossed them into boxes: the walleyes, the perch, the northern pike. The men then loaded the fish onto an old truck with a plow on the front that had been driven out onto the ice. Henry watched them set the net again and then move to another hole and pull up another net and carefully pick the fish out, so as not to tear the net. Henry watched as a cluster of men cut more blocks of ice out of the lake and loaded them onto the truck to take to the icehouses where they would be packed in sawdust. After the fish were caught and before their bodies went to the fisheries, the ice would be used to preserve them. Even at this young age, he knew his father was a hard worker. Henry watched with fascination until his mother said they must go, because it was getting too cold for Eddie. On the long way back home, Henry, the unforgettable boy who would grip the hearts of thousands, ran the snow waves as Ojibway children before him had for a thousand years.

3

Children of the Lake

Henry's parents, George and Alice, were born on opposite shores of Lake of the Woods, a secretive lake that sprawls over 1,980 miles of wilderness between the United States and Canada...a mysterious lake that opens up to no one but is part of those who are part of it...a magnificent, chilling body of water that owes its existence to the melting of a glacier two thousand years ago and is so massive that the Indians considered it four separate lakes.

A dotted line separated Lake of the Woods on maps. To the north of the dots was Manitoba, Canada; to the south, Minnesota. George was born north of the dots in 1911 in French Portage; Alice in 1912, to the south of them, in the Indian village near Warroad that has since disappeared. George's father, Joseph, was French, his mother, Rebecca, was part Cree and part Ojibway. Alice was Ojibway, raised in the traditions of her people.

George

When George was a child his father, Joseph, and his brothers built a forty-four foot freight boat which pulled a two-story barge that he had turned into a store on the lower level and a three bedroom home on the upper. Joseph filled the store with provisions from Kenora, a village on the north end of Lake of the Woods, then he would drag the well-stocked store behind the freighter to the Indian villages and fishing camps along the wild shores of the lake. The isolated people looked forward to this boat coming to bring supplies and news from other villages. Young George loved these trips with his father. He listened to the trading and the bargaining. He watched the people.

Once, when George was a small boy, he floated with his father and the houseboat/store to an Indian Pow-Wow in a remote village on the shaggy shore of the lake. As they pulled the boat into the log dock next to the canoes, George could sense the excitement. The village was already filled with Indians and some white men.

That evening, by sunset, the Pow-Wow was thick with people, dogs and an occasional horse. There were bright fires that silhouetted wigwams, and Indians dancing in the clearing. People milled and talked animatedly. Dark trees jutted behind the village, and silent animals that lived in the moist forest may have watched, but no one saw them.

Young George wandered off from his father's side to see the dancers at a closer range. Children played and ran around happily, but no one bothered him. George stood transfixed watching the Indian dancers.

Suddenly, in the midst of the festive scene, two wild stallions screamed and bolted. The people scattered, running for whatever safety they could find. Most plunged into the cold lake; some climbed trees. The horses stopped between George and where the dancers, who had taken off like winged birds, had been, and reared their gleaming bodies to fight. Like someone had flipped a tv channel on him, little George suddenly found himself watching two mighty horses preparing for battle. He tried to run, but his legs wouldn't move. The powerful stallions, with wild-burning eyes, kicked the air above them, pawed the dirt, bared their teeth, pinned their ears back, snorted and flared their nostrils like bellows before a raging fire. Little George just stood there.

Joseph felt the empty space next to him where his son should have been. Frantically he searched for him and finally saw him -- oh so dangerously near the threshing hooves. With the hair on his neck standing straight up he made a dash for his youngster, plucking him up in his strong arms like an eagle picking off a scrawny endangered offspring. Clutching him tightly to his chest, and without stopping or looking back, Joseph sprinted like a gold-bound Olympian for his boat. There, in relative safety, the anxious son and father watched in horror as the beasts fought. The horses' hooves thundered as they raised the dust and beat the earth, destroying the wigwams with their enormous bodies. For hours the stallions tore at each others' necks and slashed each others' bodies with their lethal hooves and gnashing teeth. When it was finally over one horse was a bloody victor, the other a bloody dead. The Indian camp lay demolished. George never forgot the terror that night, or the might of those horses.

Alice

Henry's mother Alice was raised by her grandmother, the medicine woman Laughing Mary Thunder, the daughter of Chief Thunder of the Buffalo Point Band. Her mother had died in the 1918 flu epidemic, when Alice was seven, and she and her doting grandmother lived together in the Indian village in Warroad.

Mary and Alice made their home in a round-topped wigwam lined with slim willow boughs and covered with bark and animal hides. In summer they would paddle a canoe forty miles north to the Windigo reserve to visit Mary's friends and relatives. Mary would steer the little craft close to the shoreline. At night they would camp under the bright stars and sleep on the soft forest floor, watched over by the animals.

In winter, when temperatures sometimes dropped to fifty below zero and the relentless wind howled outside, they wrapped in thick furs to keep warm as they huddled near the fire in the middle of their little lodge.

As soon as the ground froze, Laughing Mary told Alice Ojibway stories. You can't tell the stories until Mother Earth rests for the winter, so it was then, when Earth's white blanket covered the grasses, the fallen logs and the sleeping animals, that the Indian teachings came. Through the stories were taught courage, daring and right action; that man should neither lie nor steal; that man be moderate in speech and that man should not boast.

In the spring, when the ice melted into the warm sun's rays, it was time for prayers for the growing season: for healthy animals, abundant berries, and for the Earth to be lush green. Tobacco, made from red willow bark that had been scraped from the trees, was put into the water, assuring the fish would be plentiful.

In the warm summer, when the breezes blew soft across the waters, was the time of the Lake Ceremonies, when thanks were given to the water spirits.

When Alice was a young girl, painted Dakota/Sioux warriors came riding in on horses from the flatlands to the west. The Dakota had come to steal Ojibway horses as the Sioux had done for hundreds of years. The men of the village were away fishing. Women and children sought safe hiding places as the hooves thundered nearer. Alice and her grandmother ran to the beach of the lake and shoved off in a canoe. Unseen by the feared enemy, they paddled the canoe silently into the safety of the high green reeds that grew thickly off the shoreline. Above their thumping hearts they heard the Sioux horses, but Mary and Alice were secure in their hiding place.

In the 1920's and '30's Laughing Mary and her friends gathered cane from the river beds and willows from the nearby marshes. They wove the cane and willows into beautiful baskets. Then the Indian women would go door to door selling them in

Warroad, and sometimes they would walk as far as Roseau, Minnesota, twenty-two miles away, toting their lovely wares to locals and tourists.

Alice carried the upbringing of her devoted grandmother through her life. She was permeated with the teachings of her people which she, in turn, taught to her own children.

***

Alice and George met at a dance at French Portage in 1931 when the rest of the world was turned upside-down by the Great Depression. Shortly after the meeting, George took a creaking wooden boat from Painted Rock Narrows Fish Camp, where he lived, and sailed thirty miles back to Buffalo Bay in it. A friend fetched the Justice of the Peace, who lived twenty miles north, as the wedding feast was prepared. Word spread of the wedding celebration and fishing boats sailed in from all over the lake, anchoring off shore. A fiddler was found, food was made ready, and the wedding celebration was on.

George and Alice made their home on the shore of the great lake and raised their children on its shores as their parents had before them. The couple had nine children, one dying shortly after birth. Henry was the second-to-last child. George fished for a living and hunted for the meat they needed, and together they gathered nutritious wild rice and berries.

There were difficulties, but George and Alice, like equally yoked workhorses, set their sights toward the same end. They were industrious and steadfast, and worked hard to provide for their family.

4

By the shores of Buffalo Bay

Baby Henry was born on the first day of fishing season in 1951. His father and brothers came home to a new baby boy.

Home to little Henry was a one-bedroom cabin his father had built on a remote harbor tucked off the big bay of Buffalo Point, on the Canadian side of Lake of the Woods, nine miles northwest of Warroad. Buffalo Point was part of the southwestern end of the lake that the Indians called Pequona, which means "waters of the sand hills." The sturdy little cabin was built on a sand bar with tamarack logs that had soft green moss growing between them inside and out. It sat contented, fitting its surroundings like the last piece of a perfect puzzle. George put in a cast iron wood-burning furnace to heat it and a wood-burning stove for Alice to cook on. As a finishing touch, he added a screened-in porch as a defense against the Evil-Empire mosquitoes. (No matter how many they killed a new army of them would buzz in to take their places.) In place of electricity the Boucha family used kerosene lamps.

The snug cabin was built on Indian land. In the summer the Thunder and Lightning families lived within a few miles but in the winter no other Indians lived there. The closest neighbors to the Boucha's were the town of Warroad the nine miles to the southeast and a family of commercial fisherman, the Brewsters, of the Stoney Creek-Sandy Beach area fifteen miles to the north. The only way to reach the cabin was by water or plane in the summer, and driving the distance across the solid lake in the winter.

Henry's father built his cabin in the winter so he could haul the building materials in his green model "A" truck across the hard packed snow that covered the thick lake ice. When he finished the cabin he constructed an icehouse and filled it with blocks of the large, solid ice that he cut from the lake. George was ready to move by summer; the house was ready for the family and the icehouse was ready for the fish. He would store his daily catches on the blocks until he had enough to fill his wooden commercial fishing boat, then he would take the run to Warroad to sell them. In the summer, after the family moved in, he built a dock for the small boats; the canoes could be dragged up onto the sandy shore. His fishing boat had to be anchored about one hundred and fifty feet out into the bay.

An ancient bog flanked the cabin to the rear and the children had to be careful not to fall through the mossy top layers into the dangerous cold, acidic, spongy light brown peat that was the by-product of hundreds of years of decayed plant matter. Plump blueberries and cranberries grew in the bog.

To the left of the cabin a floating peat bog island had been driven into shore, where it was stuck for eternity. Henry's father remembered when the island moved freely in the lake, drifting as directionless as a child's lost boat. The island had been named Tamarack Island for the trees that grew on it.

Around the cove, on the skirts of the bog, was the forest. Here, on Buffalo Bay, the land was owned by the Indians and was untouched timberland. Northern white cedar that could be centuries old rested slanted and gnarled on the ancient peat. Tamaracks, the only needled tree that sheds its needles, stood a quiet vigil over the bog. Behind them the spires of black spruce pierced the sky like the spears of proud warriors. On higher ground behind the bog, majestic red and white pines, where eagles made their nests, stood silent like wise Indian chiefs, occasionally nodding with the wind and fanning the balsam fir at their knees. Groves of slender birch and quaking aspen grew on the perimeters of the forest like clusters of ghost people. In the winter the chalky birch stood bare, but in the hot summer the soft leaves gave them shade and melody as they rustled like rattlers when the wind blew through them. Graceful willow grew along the shore, their long branches swept and shook the water like the skirt of a hula dancer.

The vegetation from the rich forest offered a home and sometimes food for the animals. The fertile lake provided well for the family. Clean, clear water from the lake was used for drinking, cooking and washing. Wood to heat and cook with was abundant. The family ate walleye, perch, pike, sturgeon, and other fish from the lake including an occasional whitefish, which Alice loved boiled. The lake also provided the wild rice. Alice and George would slide into the rice field with their canoe and beat off the nutritious grain onto its wooden floor. The land provided the family with spruce grouse, deer, moose, rabbits, ducks, geese, and berries.

When the family needed venison, Henry's two oldest brothers, David and Georgie, would climb to the roof of the cabin with their guns and wait quietly for a deer to come to the edge of the forest. A moose, hunted deep within the forest, would be dried and divided between families. The meat would last a full winter. The game they took was not legal, but the family depended on it for food, and the game wardens were miles away. Once a Canadian game warden came to the cabin and saw the game but elected to look the other way. He knew George would only take what was needed for food.

What couldn't be found in the forest or lake, George brought back from Warroad by either trading the fish for food or buying what he needed in the store after selling the fish. He gave fish to friends and, in turn, friends gave him vegetables when they had extra. He traded walleye for shrimp at the fisheries. Alice fried Indian bread and a flat bread called bannock. Apples, oranges, and store-bought fruits were rare treats. There were no Cokes or candy bars.

The ever-changing lake spread out before the cabin, putting on a show for the Boucha family directed by the winds. Like a cosmic magician, it could create a perfectly smooth clear-glass mirror that stretched itself to the end of their world -- as it held its breath. Or, nymph-like, it could turn the lake choppy with frothy waves tumbling over each other. Or, like lumberjacks in a log rolling competition, it could push strong, rounded waves that rolled steadily and rhythmically onto the shore. Or, sometimes, gentle waves lapped timidly at the sand. Occasionally the magician waved his wand, unleashing lightning and thunder and wicked winds. The little family could almost hear his demonic laughter as the storms beat the little cabin, crashing the waters, bending the birch trees laterally to the earth and sending the willow hulas into mad dances.

Once, when the family was on a trip to Warroad in the big fishing boat, a hard line wind hit them. There wasn't a cloud in the sky but winds turned the lake into waves with hands. The hands of the lake churned angrily as they clawed at, clapped and swatted the big boat, whose size diminished as the water rose above them and spun them, like an erratic washing machine. George managed to turn the boat into the wind to steady it; Alice threw herself on top of Henry and Eddie. The older ones held on for their lives as the water swamped them, breathed and swamped them again...and again...and again, punching out the windows with its fingers. Then the wind stopped as suddenly as it started and the hands smoothed the water like a child patting a pet. All was calm again. The wind went on to twist trees and houses in Baudette with a force of over one hundred miles an hour.

The secluded life in the wilds of Manitoba was idyllic for the children; they could swim off the beach, run the Indian trails in the forest that had been there for hundreds of years, watch the fish swimming in the clear water above the sandy bottom and race up and down the shore for miles. They could watch the sandhill cranes, herons, eagles, hawks and owls and listen to the call of the loons and the honks of the Canadian geese. They tracked bear, lynx, wolves and foxes. They fished, picked fresh berries, and enjoyed the natural wonders of the lake and forest.

Extended family and friends from around the lake would stop by via boat in the summer and often stay overnight. Little Henry would fall asleep listening to the droning voices of the visitors after dinner, their faces back-dropped by the cozy flickering of the kerosene lamps.

When Henry was three the children at home, aside from baby Eddie, were: Jim (8), Shirley (10), David (13), and Georgie (15). There also was Purp, the faithful Chesapeake. Two older sisters, Darlene and Phyllis, were married and no longer lived at home.

There was little cause for discipline in the Boucha family as the children were busy helping their father, mother or enjoying the wilderness around them. The family was close; the feeling among them was one of warmth.

George made his livelihood with commercial fishing and some trapping, but he was dependent on the weather. If the winds whipped the lake for several days George couldn't get to his nets and the fish would rot. The winds batted the dead fish back and forth in the netting, tearing the nets with their gills. He was forced to wait for calm to drag in his 15,000 feet of net. Then came the job of emptying the fish as carefully as possible so as not to tear the nets any more than they already were. The family would sit on the shore with huge needles and mend the nets so George could fish again.

George gave Georgie and David a little piece of gill net of their own. They would paddle the blunt ended boat out from shore, set their mini net with weights, and leave it overnight. Jim and Henry would watch enviously from shore. In the mornings the boys would haul in their nets and separate their fish into boxes that George would sell for them when he went to market.

Every summer George took a two-week vacation no matter what. The whole family would load into the big boat and ride to the Boucha grandparent's farm and sawmill on the Little Grassy River. The trip was over sixty miles away – first, across the stretching, open lake, then through the thickly forested islands. They would sleep in the shrouded darkness or, if the stars were out, by the brilliant starlight. Sometimes the northern lights would splash the skies. They slept, lulled by the waves suspending the boat. Before the trip home, the family would load up with vegetables from Grandmother Rebecca's garden. In the fall she canned, and her garden kept vegetables on Henry's family's table into winter. On one of these trips, Henry's father pulled the big boat over to stop at an island so the family could picnic. The older children disembarked, climbing up the slick soft mossy rocks. Henry's little legs tried to follow suit but couldn't quite handle it. He lost his footing and skidded down the slippery vertical surface, disappearing beneath the numbing-cold iron-brown water. Alice plunged her hand under the water and grabbed. Luckily, she caught Henry's hair or he would have been lost forever beneath the boat and the waters of the hostile lake.

In winter a bush pilot would keep an eye on the settlers of the distant reaches of the lake, including the Boucha family. If there was an emergency a flag would be raised, alerting the pilot that someone was in trouble. Once, when the ice was breaking up on the lake and there was no way for George to get to town, the pilot feared the Bouchas might need meat. The family saw the plane circling above them. The good-Samaritan pilot waved as he dipped low over the cabin and dropped a ten-pound package of hamburger from the plane onto the shore by their cabin. The package broke open on earth impact and the meat spattered to kingdom come. The ground beef did make a nice meal...possibly a feast...for the small animals.

During the first years of Henry's life, he was surrounded by the friendly wilderness and a large, loving family. It was as perfect as life could be for a little boy.

Then one summer Henry's parents decided it was time to move to Warroad, the little town on the south edge of the lake. The family would come back summers, they said. Alice bought a small clapboard house on the edge of Warroad for five-hundred dollars and, when the soft summer breezes blew crisp in the evenings, the family packed their belongings into the fishing boat for the move to town.

Little Henry watched the cabin grow small as the boat pulled away from the dock of the home he loved. He watched his house, the long sandy beach and trees behind it, above the widening "V" wake the boat's engine made in the water. He watched until he could no longer see the cabin or the trees or the beach.

The comfortable little cabin George Boucha had built for his family on Lake of the Woods, the home where they had known such bliss, was washed away with high ice the following spring. The peace-filled days on the sandy shore of Buffalo Bay were forever gone for little Henry and his brothers and sister.

5

Warroad

The move to Warroad triggered a new life for tall-for-his-age Henry. His house, built on the perimeter of town, was a tiny clapboard structure sided with asphalt. The asphalt had a red brick pattern stamped into it and was rough to touch, like coarse sandpaper. The house was built on a level, treeless lot. In fact, the entire town and the earth stretching out from the west, east and south was flat, not ironed flat but flat like a blanket pulled over a lumpy mattress. Instead of a lake stretching out to the front of the generic house, a lifeless gravel street covered the earth.

Instead of a fragrant forbidden bog rich in berries, behind this house were other houses, built without grid and separated by nappy, grassy land. Houses to either side replaced the familiar forests and the soft textured woodland animals. George planted a tree. The people on the other side of the road had a cow.

The creaking floor of the wood frame house never seemed quite stable. The miniature kitchen was separate, but the rest of the house was one room. The house gained familiarity quickly because of the same good smells of Alice's cooking and the gathering of the family. A curtain separated the living room from the bedrooms: the boys all slept in one small bedroom, while sister, Shirley, had a space partitioned by another curtain. Alice hung a little hammock over her bed for baby Eddie to lie in, so when he cried at night she could put her hand up and gently rock him back to sleep.

Outside was an outhouse, which was not uncommon in the far reaches of Minnesota in the 1950's. Alice made shades out of birch bark to cover the lamps in this house that had electricity.

The Warroad River was a block and a half away from the house and flowed about a mile before it emptied into Lake of the Woods, where Alice had grown up in the Indian village. Henry was too young to go there alone, but he and his brothers ran down and threw rocks that splashed into the dark river and sunk to its bottom. When the kids tired of that, they threw sticks they could watch as they bobbed in the waves and floated out of sight.

The bustling downtown of Warroad was across the Warroad River from Henry's neighborhood. A car and footbridge went there and so did a handier railroad trestle. There was a movie theater, the train station, the Booth and Selvog fisheries, a drug store, grocery store, churches, hardware store and an unheated ice rink. The Marvin Windows Company, started in 1939, was already a strong fledgling ready to fly. In autumn, the year Henry and his family moved to town, there was still steady activity at the docks with commercial fishermen, sight-seeing boats, and large and small privately-owned boats, but the activity was winding down from the busy summer.

The Canadian National Railroad dipped out of Canada to run through Warroad before rolling back into Canada. The steam engine, trailed by a long procession of creaky freight cars, would slow down as it huffed through town. Its long, hissing sigh as it stopped, commanded the workers to service it. The engine would sit, center stage, taking on water and coal while dissecting the town in half, causing inconvenience as motorists and pedestrians waited, stranded for undeterminable amounts of time, on its wrong side. Then the long train would slowly jerk and stretch and groan its way back north, as the unstuck people scurried to their destinations.

School started. Shirley and the three older boys walked to school, leaving Henry and Eddie home all day with their mother. They weren't lonely. There was a steady stream of company. Phyllis, Henry's married sister who lived in Warroad, would visit with her baby, Billy. Members of the Buffalo Point Band, who Alice grew up with, including Kakay Geesick, "The Old Man," who was over one hundred years old, and a steady stream of members of the Thunder and the Lightning families would come to the little clapboard house. The elders, Tom Thunder, who always sat on the floor, and Tom Lightning, were also very old. When the elderly Indians would speak Ojibway with Alice, Henry would ask his mother what they were talking about in the strange tones he didn't understand. Alice's friends came for card games. Henry loved the bustle of a full house.

Alice took care of the family's medical needs. When Henry sliced his big toe nearly in two, and the toe was flip flopping back and forth, Alice poured pepper into it, squeezed it back together, and bound it firmly. The toe healed perfectly. George invested in expensive new nets and continued fishing Buffalo Bay on the Canadian side of the lake. In the winter, he also trapped so the family was snug and provided for.

This was the mid-'50's. *Bill Haley and the Comets* were rocking with *Rock Around the Clock* and a boy by the name of Elvis was making it big in the South. The Dodgers were hot, Rocket Richard ruled the hockey world and the Korean War was over. Rosa Parks had refused to give up her bus seat to a white passenger in Montgomery, Alabama. Eisenhower was president. *Rebel Without A Cause* was the big movie and Salingers' *Catcher in the Rye* was creating a mark across literary America. But, in Warroad, away from the throb of urban America, the Boucha family's main concern was adjusting to new living quarters on the perimeter of the little town. Alice's warmth made the house into a home, the older children enjoyed the movies and the music, while George's prime, cold water fish provided big city families with excellent dinners.

There was good food on the table, stability in the government, good work for George and love in his home. In the winter when the stinging winds shook the house, the cold settled and the heavy snows fell, Alice told her children the stories her grandmother had told to her, to instill a sense of responsibility and character in them.

Alice and George were respected members of the community. The Boucha family was content, nurtured and well-fed within a framework of family and friends, and little Henry, whose world was opening up, was happy.

6

Ice

When winter turned the town frigid, and the frigid turned the top water solid on the Warroad River, life changed forever for Henry Boucha. Neighborhood children rushed by the little Boucha house on the way to the river to ice skate. Georgie, David, Shirley and Jim watched these children out of their window and begged their mother for ice skates. Alice went on a mission, managing to round up hand-me-down ice skates for all the older children, including four-year-old Henry. Eddie was too little to go out yet.

The first pair of skates Henry had were at least three sizes too big for him. Alice told him to put on as many pairs of socks as he could, and then she stuffed more socks inside the toe. None of the Boucha flock knew how to skate, so everyone did their share of falling down. All the siblings: Georgie, David, Jim, Shirley, and faithful Purp were responsible for watching Henry when they skated on the river. The older brothers and sister did not think of this as a hardship. It was just part of being a large family.

There were no skating lessons! The boy, only a few years out from becoming a legend in United States hockey; who sent chills down the spines of anyone who saw him skate; who was remembered years after his career was over, as the most fluid and self-assured skater anyone had ever seen...never had a skating lesson.

Road hockey was the second love of the Warroad boys. The streets would freeze over with thick, uneven ice. The boys built make-shift goals in the middle of the street and would play hockey for hours. A flattened tobacco can was used as a puck, and sometimes the boys would tape catalogues on their legs for protection from the sting of being smacked by a hard-hit can.

Whenever the older kids needed a goalie for playing road hockey in front of the Boucha house, they would ask Henry's mom if Henry could be their goalie. She usually said yes and would dress him up warmly. He would stand in goal for the older kids and come back inside full of welts and bruises. The good thing about Henry -- in the eyes of the older kids -- was that he didn't cry very much and never complained and was always game to go out and do it again. This was his start of playing with older boys.

The boys, including Henry, skated to school on the bumpy, brownish-yellow iced roads that didn't thaw for many months.

Henry's early childhood was filled with happy days: a very special mother who loved her brood; a father who was proud of his work and who worked hard for his family; cohesive brothers and sisters; and a network of friends who respected him. The nucleus of his hockey career, though certainly not at a jelled stage, was already forming.

PART II

LATER CHILDHOOD

AGEWATE..."THERE IS A SHADOW"
OJIBWAY

7

First shadows

Henry started kindergarten when he was five. On the first day of school, Henry's mother told him he was going to school. He wanted to know why. Alice told him it was to learn. "How do I learn?" he questioned. "You'll know," Alice assured him. He had his little rug to nap on and loved the milk breaks because at home his family drank powdered milk. Henry liked playing with all the kids. Kindergarten was a success.

The next year his older brother Georgie left for the Navy without finishing school. Sixteen-year-old David, Jim now eleven, Shirley who was thirteen and little Henry walked across the bridge of the Warroad River to the little school with the spread-winged stone eagle perched over the door. Georgie's absence left the others with the feeling of the first leaf of fall leaving the branch. It was inevitable, but earlier than expected, and left a sad void. David, in losing his best friend and brother, became despondent and restless.

In the winter the skating resumed on the Warroad River. Henry could scoot all over the ice by now. When the big boys played hockey they used him as their goalie. He took his goal-tending post seriously, was quick and became surprisingly proficient at stopping their pucks. Henry felt that if he had to play goalie for the big kids then he would be the best that he could. He developed an uncanny concentration from playing this position.

Henry played hockey with his older brothers, Jim and David, and their friends and other boys he knew from school and the neighborhood. He spent hours playing ice hockey on the river or road hockey on the ever ice-coated winter roads near the house. Gary Sargent, who became an NHL player later in his life, was one of the children involved in these games.

Except for Georgie's absence and David's unsettled feeling, the sun still warmed the Boucha family. George made what they considered a solid living gill netting in the Canadian waters of Buffalo Bay. He had a pride in what he did and he did it well. One day a child at school told Henry his family was poor. That night Henry asked his dad if they were poor. "You bet we are!" George answered with a big twinkling smile and that was the end of that. Alice was happy with her family and friends. The family was as tight as the lid on grandma's preserves.

upside-down

Then, in the summer of 1957, without warning, gill netting was declared illegal in the Canadian waters of Lake of the Woods. George lost his commercial (Canadian) fishing license and, because he was not a U.S. citizen, was not able to get a U.S. license. In that move over which he had no control, Henry's father lost his sense of who he was. George had fished his entire life. He was good at what he did; he was proud of what he did. Not only had he supported his family, the family's entire life revolved around his commercial fishing business. All his assets were tied up in boats and equipment. As quickly as the tip of the red sun sinks beyond our sight, George's psyche snapped, numbing part of him forever.

Disorientated, George became bitter and turned to drinking. Instead of the upbeat, self-assured man that was his father, Henry saw a different, sullen man-shell in his place. It didn't take long for the family to fill with anxiety and fear. The brightness faded from Alice's ever-smiling face. She started working to make ends meet. As she was uneducated, it was menial work and it exhausted her. It was a difficult time for Alice who tried to keep the family going.

The first shadows flung themselves across Henry's life when he was six years old. The little boy's idyllic life, and the peace and joy that went with it, was over.

8

Georgie

David, knowing the financial hardships facing his father, knew he had to leave home. It would be one less mouth for his father to worry about. He followed Georgie's footsteps to the service before finishing high school. Shirley, Jim, Henry and little Eddie missed him. Half the Boucha children had left the nest. Darlene, the oldest, was living in Idaho with her husband and children. Phyllis was married and living in Warroad with her family.

Georgie was visiting Darlene in Idaho. David was in the Navy in Texas. The children at home missed their older brothers and they missed their happy father and the well-being he had given them. They missed their mother's cheerfulness and hated the edge this strain had put on her. The gray shadows pressed down on them like thick fog in a dense forest and it was hard for them to get their bearings.

murder

The third shadow came black and angry sweeping across the family blotting out any sun. In September of 1959 when Henry was eight, Darlene's husband Jim's niece was in a bad marriage and had decided, for safety reasons, that she had to leave her volatile husband. Darlene offered visiting Georgie to help her move out. The girl's husband came home and saw Georgie moving his wife's things out of the house. Without finding out what was going on, or who Georgie was, he whipped out a gun and shot Georgie. When Georgie was down, he shot him again. There was no question about it; the second shot was premeditated murder.

Alice and George were devastated at the death of their son. Darlene came back on the train, bringing Georgie's body. It was with broken hearts that the family laid Georgie to rest.

The man who shot Georgie was never convicted. His lawyers pleaded self-defense; Georgie had no weapon. Georgie was very large, strong and intimidating, and in Idaho the law read that a man could protect his home -- and that is the argument the lawyer used. The kangaroo court jumped on that one. It didn't help that he was Indian and the man who shot him was white.

David, in the service in Texas, was notified he had to go home because his brother had been killed. He was not informed *which* brother. David rode the lonely bus north for two days not knowing which brother was dead. When he got home, Henry, little Eddie and Jim were sitting on the sofa, and this is how David knew which brother he would never see again.

The cruel and senseless murder of Georgie and the ensuing unfair trial took an enormous toll on the family.

9

The making of a legend

If a person hasn't actually felt it, he or she cannot know the oppressiveness of sub-zero cold. To those who have, it is never forgotten. When wind is injected into the freezing air, it becomes the aggressor -- whipping the snow, plant life, animals and humans with fury. These winds take on an eerie aliveness. The winds that blew across the winter northern prairies were as menacing to the modern inhabitants of Warroad as the Sioux warriors a century before who had come riding across the plains to harass the Ojibway. The cold came like a weight and held the inhabitants of Warroad in a cocoon for months, and when the winds came they batted any inhabitant who ventured outside, so they stayed inside as much as possible.

The Warroad boys seemed to have immunity against the elements. They would be out in force; skating the river, the ponds, on ditches, the old arena, homemade ice rinks in people's yards, or playing road hockey with their boots on and using a smashed chewing tobacco can that was weighted for a puck.

Some of the boys might have been out some of the time; but with Henry it was all the time. He skated after school and evenings and all day weekends...always perfecting his stride and always working on his speed. His teachers were himself and watching the older boys. He usually played with boys older than he was and always had to work harder to keep up. No one told Henry to work, no one told Henry to skate. No one told Henry he had to practice. No one taught him how to stick handle or how to shoot. Henry was his own teacher; the older boys were his sparring partners.

As soon as a pond would freeze, Henry and a smattering of other boys would anxiously watch the ice for when it could hold them. As soon as there was a layer as thick as a piece of plate glass the kids would dare each other to skate on it. Henry would take off and hear the ice cracking with his weight and skate back as fast as he could for the safety of shore.

The Warroad River was the favorite place to skate. When the ice formed thick, there was no better place to play hockey. It was best when the ice froze before it snowed because then the whole river was their empire. They could skate up and down its lid for miles playing hide and seek or tag.

At night there were shadows from the town's lights shining on the ice and the boys could see silhouettes of people. They loved it when the moon was full and bright, illuminating them like actors on a stage. Sometimes they would build bonfires to warm themselves and light the river. From the bridge, the fires looked like stationary fireflies flickering in the darkness.

When he skated on the river, Henry would go back and study the patterns his blades carved through the ice or snow: how even they were, how smooth they were, their length. Even at this young age, he was striving for excellence.

***

One time Henry and his brother, Jim, were playing hockey on the river. It was very, very cold and Henry wasn't wearing a hat. He and Jim were down there a long time when Jim saw that Henry's ears were frozen. Henry went home to show his mother, who was shocked to see the pure white ears. Henry had to stay indoors. As the ears thawed they started to sting and hurt so badly Henry was crying in pain. The ears swelled about three sizes too big and Henry had to stay home from school. After a day or two they felt better but started peeling. Henry didn't mess with nature again. He always wore a hat.

Lyle Kvarnlov's, who later played with Henry on his high school team, father owned a grocery store with a meat market in the back. When the kids, including Frank Krahn, Robert Storey, and Jeff Hallet, would get a new stick they would run to Lyle's father's store. Mr. Kvarnlov would always put aside what he was doing to trim down the ends of the hockey sticks for the enthusiastic, beaming-eyed little boys -- with his meat saw blade. Then he would swing another pork chop on the saw!

Mr. Kvarnlov, ever the good father, flooded his yard with water every winter so the kids could skate. Pucks would get lost in the deep snow, not to be found until spring. The little boys didn't have a goalie stick. The only substitute they could find was a scoop shovel. No one wanted to play goalie because the puck would come off the shovel and hit the unlucky goalie in the face. One year the boys decided to burn the high grass off the yard to help Lyle's father get the space cleared for the rink. It all started innocently until a wind came up, fanning the flames ten feet in the air in the direction of the neighbor's house. The little boys watched as the fire department hosed down the flames close to the frantic neighbor's home.

In the event Henry was not skating or playing a form of hockey, he would find other amusements. In winter, he and Bob

Wenzel, who would also play high school hockey with Henry, would hitch rides on the back of the milk truck's bumper until the driver chased the offenders away. Or, they would go to the river and jump off the wall into the snow banks below...or trek across the frozen river to Government Island and make snow forts, sneaking around spying on other kids doing the same thing. They were kids being kids. Wednesday nights everyone watched Hockey Night in Canada -- in black and white -- on the only channel Warroad got, and everyone wanted to be Frank Mahovlich. Sometimes Henry would tag along with his older brother Jim when he trapped. Jim made good money at it, but it was a long walk for Henry so he didn't go often. Jim trapped wolf, fox, mink, rabbit, beaver and muskrat.

***

The boys rarely missed a Warroad Warriors High School hockey game or a Lakers semi-pro hockey game. They would help scrape the rink for a free pop and run around under the bleachers when they weren't watching the action. The Warroad rink, affectionately dubbed "The Barn" by the other teams who came to play in it, and called "The Garden" by Warroad residents, had been built by volunteer labor except for the head carpenter, Ed Christian, who was the father of hockey players Billy, Roger and Gordon Christian. Since it was a community effort, the kids never had to pay to play.

When Henry was nine, Norwegian and Finnish teams came to the little town to play the Warroad Lakers. The Norwegians came to the school and sang to the children in Norwegian. To Henry this was awesome.

Later that year, Roger and Billy Christian were selected to the 1960 U.S. Olympic team that won the Gold Medal that year in Squaw Valley, California. This wasn't lost on Henry who was taking it all in.

With Henry it wasn't a desire to copy the older boys. They were fun to watch but Henry was enamored with skating and knew intuitively that with work and practice he would be one of the blazing players of the high school himself one day. He even dreamed of being on the U.S.A. Olympic team. Henry loved the feeling of riding the ice...the faster the better. When the kids chased each other and played hide and seek around Government Island in the high reeds that stuck out of the frozen lid of the lake, he was on another plane, where he wanted to live and be, and spend eternity.

When Henry was nine the family couldn't afford skates for him. Alice and George decided Henry wouldn't play hockey that year. John Parker, the game warden, came to the Boucha house to find out where Henry was when he didn't show up for his team sign-up. When John found out why Henry wasn't there he went uptown and bought a pair of skates for Henry. That is the kind of person John Parker was!

When Henry was eleven he played defense on the Peewee team and tended goal for Warroad's Bantam team (the thirteen to fifteen-year-olds). The jerseys were sweatshirts. Each player painted PEEWEES on them big and bold across the front. The games would be back-to-back. Henry would dress for the Peewee game, play that contest and then go to the locker room and put on his goalie equipment for the Bantam game -- right over his Peewee equipment. Dick Roberts, who would later become his high school coach, coached the Bantam team. Henry made Dick Roberts nervous because he blew bubble gum and the bubbles grew so huge Roberts was afraid Henry wouldn't be able to see the pucks coming! Roberts would yell at Henry from the bench to tone down the bubbles.

That spring the Bantam team traveled to Winnipeg, Canada, where a kid from Swift said, "Hey, there goes one of them-there electric deals." It was an electric bus. The kid's hick declaration left everyone in stitches.

Roberts also arranged for them to go to a tournament in Colorado. It was exciting for everyone to travel away from home to play hockey.

***

The next year Henry skated "out," on defense. Roberts managed to get eighteen games for his players. They lost only two of the games that season. When the Bantam team played in Thief River Falls, against the Thief River Bantam team, Huck Olson, sports columnist of the *Thief River Falls Times*, and Bud Brussoit, who had played in the first state high school hockey tournament in St. Paul, Minnesota in 1945, were in attendance. Huck said to Bud as they were watching Henry, "That kid has a wrist!" He went on to note what a great skater Henry was. Huck predicted to Bud that Henry would be a great player some day. "Unbelievable," was the label Bud, himself, put on Henry at that age. Henry was clearly a rising star when he was in the 6th grade.

The Bantams played the Edina Bantam team, who had played fifty-four games and also lost only two, for the State Bantam Championship. Edina was favored to win. Warroad upset Edina for the Bantam title.

Roberts knew Henry was a fine and solid player but, in the Edina-Warroad State Bantam Championship game, he caught the brilliance of what was to come. "Edina had an excellent center, Bob Kreiger, who later was a star player for Denver University. During the game Kreiger came in on Henry at the blue line, deeked him slick and clean and went around Henry toward the goal. Henry wheeled around and caught the player before he could shoot and knocked the puck away. As the saying goes, he could spin on a dime and be at full speed in two strides." (Quote from Dick Roberts in his presentation speech for Henry when he was inducted into the U.S. Hockey Hall of Fame.)

***

Henry got an early label as being a "rink rat" -- a child that would be skating almost every waking hour. It was this tenacity, this ice time...this desire to skate, skate, skate and to be better, better, better that propelled him. It was a little light burning inside him that was the most important thing in his life and he never wanted it to go out.

10

Being Indian

When Henry grew old enough to go to the movies (somewhere between eight and nine-years-old), it struck him that being Indian was not the "right" thing to be. In those days the Indian children had nothing to be proud of. They would watch John Wayne and other "westerns" where the Indians never won and were portrayed as drunk and stupid.

Henry went through a phase of being ashamed of his heritage. When the other Indian families, who lived in and around Warroad, would come to visit the Boucha family, the kids would play together...and *all* the kids spoke only English. The adults would speak Ojibway (also known as Chippewa), but the language Henry had loved to hear his mother speak when he was a child took on a new, harsh light for him. He, and the other Indian children, in order to protect themselves in the white world where they needed to survive, branded the Indian language as "dumb" (distancing themselves from it), and never learned it. When Henry saw his mother's relatives or the other Indian families, he was embarrassed and didn't want to be anything like them. He would pretend he wasn't an Indian, or sometimes he would just leave to go find his white friends.

1 1

Phyllis

In 1963 when the Flower Children were descending on San Francisco, Henry was an eleven-year-old living in the slow-changing reaches of Minnesota. George had added a room to the house for much-needed space. Life was now a mixed bag for Henry. He had the home environment of a loving family, but his parents were grieving Georgie; were stressed out financially; and they were worred about David, who was in S.E. Asia in the Vietnam conflict.

Henry's older sister, Phyllis, had four young children now. One, Billy, had a fascination with matches. When Shirley was seventeen and in high school, she was baby-sitting for older sister Phyllis' children and older brother Jim's baby. When Phyllis came home Shirley decided that instead of going back home, she would just spend the night there with Phyllis at her house. Shirley went to sleep in a bedroom on the second floor.

Billy, the oldest child, got up very early -- unknown to the sleeping household -- and went right for the matches. Before he knew it the house was on fire and spreading rapidly, having ignited the old oil-burning heater. Phyllis, and Henry's brother Jim's baby's mother, Marlys, managed to get everyone out of the house...except Shirley who was trapped upstairs. The flames lashed at Shirley and she couldn't get out down the fiery stairwell. Her hands and face were being seared as the house turned into an inferno. Seeing no other option, Shirley flung herself out a window, landing on the hard packed snow above the solidly frozen ground. She broke he nose and arm. Fortunately she had protective clothing on, including a sweatshirt and blue jeans, or the burn damage would have been even worse. Shirley, who was lucky to escape alive, spent three months in the hospital recuperating from the burns and still carries the scars thirty years later.

Phyllis relocated her family to a little two-bedroom, one-story house. Henry was awakened one night by the shrill, demanding scream of fire engines. He lay awake with the chilled feeling something was very wrong. When the phone rang in their house his mother knew, too; she asked his father to answer the phone. Billy, who couldn't have been more than five or six, was playing with matches in the basement again. When the fire started he and Jeff, an even younger brother who was with him, managed to run to safety, but Phyllis and the two babies were caught inside.

Phyllis was pulled out, barely alive, with third-degree burns over 80% of her body. She was found in the bathtub, trying to find her toddlers that she could hear screaming. The firemen found their lifeless bodies in a closet. After two agonizing weeks in the burn center in Minneapolis, Phyllis couldn't hang on anymore. She died, leaving a grieving Boucha family behind.

***

In the summer of 1963, outside of Warroad, the world was in upheaval. Oppressed Black Americans were fighting for human rights; Martin Luther King delivered the landmark, *I Have a Dream,* speech; Bob Dylan, who would be labeled, "the voice of the generation," was singing *Blowin' in the Wind* and *The Times They Are A-Changin.'* The Vietnam Conflict was escalating. Kennedy was President...and then suddenly, in the fall of 1963, he wasn't. He had been brutally shot, and the world, including Henry, felt the shock.

In Henry's world he was twelve. He had witnessed the transformation of his self-sufficient father into a disorientated, bitter man due to the forced end of his business. He had also seen a profound change in his mother due to hard work outside the home and dealing with the change in his father. He had seen both of his parents grieve the loss, through death, of their children and grandchildren. Henry, himself, had felt the tragedy of the death of his brother and his sister, his cousins *and* the affable President.

Like a trigger pulled and a shot fired that could not be recouped, Henry's family's life fired in a direction they didn't want to go and there was nothing they could do about it. There was nothing that could bring back George's fishing license and restore his self-respect as a self-employed fisherman on the lake he knew so well. There was nothing that could bring back Georgie and Phyllis or the President. The sadness and the change was final.

***

In his personal life, Henry was developing into an athlete. He was a sandlot standout in baseball. In hockey he had the feeling of being a capable goalie beyond his years and playing on a team with older boys who treated him like an equal. He kept working on his skating by perfecting his stride and his speed. Henry loved the ice. He loved the feeling of skating fast. He loved hockey.

PART III

HIGH SCHOOL

WASSEBAGISGJA ANANG... "THE STAR IS BRIGHT, SHINING"
OJIBWAY

12

Warriors

When Henry was in the 8th grade (the junior high was in the same complex as the grade school), the town of Warroad was hockey crazy. As early as 1948, Native American Max Oshie, was blazing his name, and Warroad's, into state tournament play-books. Warroad does not carry the name "Hockey Town U.S.A." without reason! In 1958 Warroad had been represented with five members on the U.S. National Team: the three Christian brothers and Dan McKennan as players and Cal Marvin as coach. For the varsity games, the fans would pack the old "barn" arena shoulder to shoulder. To play on the varsity team was a privilege and the boys who did were held in high esteem.

Henry was a tall, gangly kid by this time and hung with a confident aura. He was voted class president.

Grafstrom

Myron Grafstrom was Warroad's (rather young) high school coach. He came from the tiny town of Salo and had played high school hockey in nearby Roseau. He graduated in '51 (the year Henry was born), joined the Army and, after he came back, played for the University of Minnesota. That was in '57, '58, and '59. (His teammates included Murray Williamson, Jerry Norman of Eveleth, Oscar Mahle of International Falls and Larry Johnson of Edina.)

Grafstrom was surprised that Warroad didn't have the number of kids out for hockey that Roseau did, but Warroad was a tiny town and the *numbers* just weren't there. He found out that Warroad was able to field competitive teams because the few players they did have were excellent.

Henry was on the Junior B high school squad but Grafstrom also placed Henry's name on the varsity roster. Grafstrom didn't expect to play Henry much (he was 5th defenseman) but he planned to work him in on easy games so he would be a little bit experienced for next year when he would be a freshman.

It was a big deal for Henry to dress with the varsity team in the tiny dressing room that held so much prestige. Henry sat on the bench through the first few games. He was waiting patiently for his break. As Coach Grafstrom looked down the bench, he knew Henry wanted to play. His eyes were so bright and he was so eager; he was just a delight for the coach to have sitting there.

Warroad always seemed to be one defenseman short. The big defensemen on the Warroad team that year were David Foster, Gordy Huerd, John Roberts -- who went on to West Point -- and Vern Hodgson. (Vern's father was Canadian. His grandfather came to Warroad during the war to work in the factory that made cartons for packing ammunition.) Jim Jaros and Buzz Marvin were the strong forwards. Duane Foster was the goalie.

Henry was "in" now and playing with the big guys as he had since he was little -- but now it was official. His illustrious high school hockey career had started and he wasn't even in high school yet.

One of the drills Grafstrom ran was his cone drill. He would place two cones on each blue line. The player would skate out to the pylon, face the boards and stop, then pivot to the right. After making this first circle the player would skate to the next cone facing away from the boards turning to the left, and wheel around the pylons, skating tight around it (doing a spin turn) carrying the puck. Then he would go to the next blue line and repeat the routine, then skate on to take a shot on net. Henry excelled at that drill. He would skate out enthusiastically, pretty much full speed, and spin low and close to the cones, like A.J. Foyt hugging the inside lane on the Brickyard corners. He always had good body balance, wrapping the cone tightly with his body as he held on to the puck with his stick. Even as an eighth-grader he did that drill better than anyone; so smooth, so fast and with such concentration. Henry was always serious about hockey. He worked hard at practice and did the drills as meticulously as he could...always, always striving for perfection. He never dogged the drills.

Defenseman John Roberts would take naps before the games and would sometimes oversleep. Henry got excited every time this happened because he thought John wouldn't show up and he, Henry, would get lots of ice time. John always showed up, of course, shattering Henry's ice-dreams.

When the team played their arch rival, Roseau, the consistent you-could-bet-on-it powerhouse team, it was tense. And, when the Warriors played in Roseau, they would pile on the bus and sit white-faced and white-knuckled for the twenty-two mile bus ride across the flattened northern prairies with the snow stretching in all directions like an old bleached tarp. It was serious business: like they were going to war. The two times the team played Roseau in regular season play each year were always critical. Both teams played at a higher rung, and the anxious fans bit their nails and lived with butter-churn stomachs until the board read its final score.

debut

The team was playing Roseau. Grafstrom hadn't played the 8th grader yet. He certainly wasn't planning on it against Roseau. Henry was sitting on the bench, where he had sat so far this season, intently involved in watching the game...itching to be out there...always waiting for his break...and ready for it when it came.

A Warroad defenseman got a penalty. The other two defensemen were tired, having just had their shift. Grafstrom looked down the bench and saw the eager Henry with his "let me out there" look. Roseau had a man advantage; this certainly wasn't the time to put out the rookie junior high kid, but Grafstrom found himself signaling Henry onto the ice. There was not a second of hesitation from Henry...he saw the waited-for signal as clearly as his Indian brave fore-brothers had seen their signal in the hunt so many years before...and he reacted just as swiftly. He jumped over the boards and onto the ice. He would show the coach his moves; the moves he had worked on since he was a little boy. There was a job to be done and Henry knew he was the man to do it.

The puck came back to young Henry at his own blue line. He caught it as a burly Roseau veteran zoomed in on his prey -- the novice 8th grade kid: Henry. Henry could have dumped the puck. He could have muffed it and everyone would have chalked it up to first-time jitters. He could have panicked and the fans would have said, in kindness, that the youngster needed experience. Instead, young Henry cooly faked a shot and spun away from the Roseau guy leaving the astonished fore-checker standing there like *Coyote* tricked by the *Roadrunner*. Then with the confidence of a seasoned varsity player, he went to center ice and lopped the puck into the other zone. The fans and his coach got their first taste of the thrills that were to come. And the coach never forgot it. Grafstrom knew Henry was headed for the heights of the hockey world.

Quote from Myron Grafstrom in recalling this thirty years later:
"Imagine! The very first varsity shift, a man short, and against the powerhouse Roseau! Very impressive for a kid who just stepped on varsity ice for the first time."

Henry's teammates already knew about Henry...they had seen these moves on the river and the ponds. But there was no question about it: Henry gained renewed respect of the players and every person watching the game that night. The story of the legend had begun.

Henry played regular shifts after that, wowing the crowds with his prowess, fancy moves and speed. The team had a good record that year. They lost to their nemesis Roseau in the playoffs and did not make it to the coveted state tournament that year. Roseau was a bigger city and always had more depth.

For Henry it was a great year. He established himself and his skills firmly and had four more years of high school to play.

***

Hockey season only lasted from December through March. Henry had to condense his mini-hockey season into mega-doses of skating everywhere he could (rinks, the ditches, the river, the gravel pit) for three and a half months. He submerged himself in hockey and skating. There was no spring hockey or summer hockey or fall hockey. There were no fancy hockey camps in the summer for Henry to go to with big name pro players running them. International tournaments filled with All-Star teams hadn't hit the hockey scene yet. There would be no politically connected father behind him cracking the whip or paying off the teams so Henry could play. The incredible thing about Henry is that he did it all on his own. Somewhere inside him was a ticking clock that knew what he had to do to become the best. On his own he skated outdoors, and in Grafstrom's practices he made use of every second.

goodbye

Myron Grafstrom was in Warroad for a three-year stint. He taught science and coached track and hockey. This was the third year of his contract. The next year he got a job offer in the twin cities suburb of Bloomington as the first hockey coach for Bloomington-Jefferson.

***

George was working for Heinen, a mink ranch in Warroad, in the winter, and continued working as a fisherman for Dorrance and Alvin Johnston fishing with trawlers for fish food for the minks in the summer. He also trapped animals to make extra money. Alice was working an energy-sapping, humdrum job at the Warroad Hospital.

Henry was close to both parents, but especially Alice, who kept the sense of family that Laughing Mary had taught her during the long winters, the beautiful springs, the lingering summers and the glorious falls of the border country. Henry had an exemplary upbringing from Alice and later, when life's elastic pulled as far as it could stretch in the stressful world of the white man, Henry Boucha snapped back to the real center of what is important in life...just as Alice had taught him.

13

Indian Rising

When Henry was in the 9th grade (the high school was housed in the same complex as the grade school and junior high), a new coach came to town from Bemidji State College where he had played hockey. His name was John Hopkins. His background was Canadian. He was twenty-one-years old and rarin' to go. John Hopkins was from the "new school," was very innovative and a disciplinarian.

John was also Henry's physical education teacher. In the fall he ran indoor dry land drills to get all the athletes ready for their sports and the other boys in condition. John noted that Henry instinctively knew how to use his body to protect the puck.

When hockey practices started, John Hopkins made the goalies run with goalie pads on when the team was running distances. Since Henry played both goalie and defense the coach hadn't decided where to play him, but when the team ran races and Henry beat everyone John figured out quickly that Henry would be a fast skater and that was the end of Henry's goalie career forever. That year Henry played forward at the beginning of the season and then Hopkins, realizing Henry's ability to see the play developing, put him on defense so Henry could see the whole ice. Hopkins believed in building the defense first and then taking it from there. There was no doubt about it. Henry was an ice-hummer and Hopkins was delighted to have this boy on his team.

The "downtown quarterbacks" were also excited about their good fortune in Henry. He was their pride and joy: their big gun from Bantams who had turned into a cannon by 8th grade. They wanted the team built around this amazing athlete. The townspeople felt, with Henry doing most of the team's work, that they had a chance to go to State. They felt the way to do this was to play Henry all the time and they let Hopkins know this.

Hopkins saw it differently. He wanted to build a team where all the kids contributed. He felt that playing Henry all the time would cause friction on the team and with the other parents. He also felt that a fourteen-year-old boy didn't need the pressure of being a one man team and that a kid that age, no matter how good he was, wanted to fit in — not be singled out. John was working on total self-esteem, not just focusing on athletic self-esteem, for his players. He felt the "quarterbacks" wanted to win at all costs, no matter what it did to the athlete, and he just didn't agree with this.

At a young age Henry had a very special presence on the ice. People were drawn to watch him. As a freshman in high school Henry had the same attraction in the halls at school that he had on the ice. He dressed differently from the others, neater – almost preppy. The other boys dressed more relaxed – almost scruffy. He marched to a different drum from his classmates, but maintained a boyish likeableness and certainly a charisma.

Henry had a catchy enthusiasm about him. He was always humble, quiet and always a positive force for John Hopkins.

During ice season Henry didn't let up with always practicing to be better. He was still constantly on the river and the ditches, and, now that he was older, the gravel pit. He was constantly working on his skills...working, working in the bitter cold that was always built into the northern Minnesota winters. The light in him that wanted to excel, to be the best, was burning warm.

***

John Hopkins ran a drill that he called a shinny drill. Everyone was on the ice and John would toss a puck in the midst of the players. Everyone had to try to get this one puck, play keep-away with it and hang on to it as long he could. The kids liked the drill. John would play it with them. Once John and Henry were fighting for the puck and in the excitement John's stick whacked Henry's forehead. It gave Henry quite a goose-bump. John told Henry to keep his head up!

It was an interesting year for Henry. He was already a blossoming star athlete in football, baseball and hockey. As such, he was carving out a niche for himself in the town. The people admired him and pinned their hopes on him for a state hockey championship.

games

The year was a good one for the Warroad Warriors hockey team. They played the usual Region 8 teams and also played Robinsdale, a suburb of Minneapolis.

Warroad and Roseau both beat each other in regular season play, each winning on their home ice.

Serge Gambucci was the renowned coach at Grand Forks, North Dakota, High School. When his team came to play

Warroad, his team was ahead by one goal. Time was running out and the Warroad timekeeper stopped the clock to buy time for the Warriors. Gambucci showed his wrath by pounding on the clock with a hockey stick.

When Robinsdale came up to play it was assumed that the Warriors would cream them, but Robinsdale caught them napping and beat them. This upset Henry, who took losses to heart. This hatred of losing was one of the things that *tuned* Henry into being successful.

After every game Hopkins would say, "Where are we going?" and the boys would answer, "We're going to State." He would say it again and they would answer louder. He would say it again and they would yell it at the tops of their lungs.

On a personal level John liked the quiet, serious, outstanding player, Henry, and Henry liked John Hopkins. Henry did see a lot of ice time his freshman year; Hopkins was no fool! He used young Henry on the power play and the penalty kill.

Excitement for the hockey team was running high that year. They were a winning team. The people of Warroad wanted a State Championship team but it seemed to John Hopkins that they wanted it at any cost. The talent and coaching was more than adequate, they had a budding superstar and the town sensed that they had a run at it. All season, the coveted tournament tantalized them and teased them like an exotic dancer. It was a curious time of ebbing and flowing that lasted the duration of the hockey season. The ups and downs of the town were cemented to the scores of the games that winter.

The town was so integrated into hockey that Hopkins would go to church and the sermon would be about last night's game. He would go to the Legion and be besieged by just about everyone in town telling him how to run his team, or at least offering advice. Dick Roberts would come and pick him up for a ride and give Hopkins pointers on how to coach. John couldn't even go to the grocery store or bank without people telling him what to do. The young coach took this all in stride and held to his principles and ran his team his way despite the barrage of helpers. The one person John looked forward to coming to help him out on the ice was Billy Christian, who had developed into a quiet, soft-spoken young man who taught the kids some tricks from his 1960 Gold Medal Team Olympic days. All in all there was a magic to the team. The team felt it, the coach felt it, the town felt it.

John Hopkins played with the Warroad semi-pro Lakers

hockey team for awhile. The Warriors played against the Lakers in a few scrimmages which helped develop the Warriors. Henry was always amazed how the "older guys" could move the puck so well. They had the kids running around. Experience always won out; the young pups never did beat the Lakers.

The Warriors won the Conference Title. Now all they had to do was win the two games in region playoffs. Warroad won the first game easily....now a mere one game was between them and the State Tournament.

Henry, a force on the team, was ready for the big show in St. Paul, Minnesota. The big game to determine who would represent Region 8 at the Minnesota State High School Tournament was held in Roseau against Roseau...anything but neutral ground! The scant twenty-two miles that separated the two towns insured a serious rivalry rarely paralleled in any sports history. It could be likened to USC vs. UCLA football perhaps, but the point is it was always fierce.

The Warriors had beaten the Roseau Rams earlier in the season and went into the playoffs with an impressive 18-4 record.

front door

Roseau was coached by a legend of its own...Oscar Almquist. Oscar was from the old school...no fooling around. He was in charge of his team. Oscar Almquist was very disciplined and highly respected; he was one of the best coaches ever in Minnesota high school hockey. Oscar taught his players to head-man the puck, he taught them teamwork and to open up the ice and to let the puck do the work through passing. John Hopkins respected Oscar Almquist.

When John Hopkins would go to Roseau to buy clothes the people were always very cordial to him, especially radio sports announcer, Bernie Bergraff, who also owned a clothing store in Roseau.

That year Roseau had three big guns of their own: Brian Grand, who went on to play college hockey at Bemidji State – (and who later played on a U.S. National team with Henry); the large and imposing Mike Baumgartner, who went on to play for North Dakota and the Chicago Blackhawks; and Blaine Comstock, who played for Bemidji State and also on the '76 Olympic team. Roseau had three well-balanced lines.

In the first period Warroad outshot Roseau. John Hopkins

was pleased and told his players to keep shooting. During the next two periods the Warriors wore down like old shoe soles. The spunky Rams stayed on Henry, tying him up at every opportunity. Billy Poole, cousin of Joe and Jack Poole, rip-roaring stars of mid-'50's hockey from Thief River Falls, was the Warroad goalie. He was doing a brisk business blocking shots, but four got past him and Warroad only managed a lone goal. Roseau would be the Region 8 representative. It was Henry's first experience of a bitter loss. They blew it, and on what seemed a *very* long bus trip back to Warroad, no one said anything.

back door

The Warriors had another chance to go to the state tournament as the Region 3 representative. Region 7 and Region 8 second place teams played each other to go to the state tournament as the Region 3 representative. It was called going through the "back door." This second-chance game was also played in Roseau that year. It was close for the Warriors but their opponents, Greenway-Coleraine, had to come two hundred miles by bus. Highly respected Bob Genander was the coach. The stands were packed up shoulder-to-shoulder with fans brought in by the busloads from Greenway-Coleraine and Warroad. Early in the first period Henry got the puck in the slot and flipped a brilliant shot on the stick side. He didn't get all of it but the goalie didn't move. The puck was in and the score was 1-0 Warroad! The crowd roared.

The exciting contest -- a great defensive battle -- tied 2-2 at the end of regulation play.

overtime!

About two minutes into the overtime, with everyone's hearts beating in their mouths, Warroad's forward George Ganyo broke loose on a breakaway. He deeked the goalie and beat him! The pack was on its feet. The players in the box were on their feet. Henry and John Hopkins were already on that bus to St. Paul. Ganyo slid the puck in backhand.... He got a little too much pull on it but it sailed behind the goalie!

The Warroad section was jumping up and down like popcorn in a kettle: cheering, yelling, celebrating! The puck hit the post, went sliding across the back of the goalie -- this side of the blue line -- hit the other post and spurted back out into play.

No goal! No goal!

John Hopkins just about jumped out of his underwear. Henry stared, not believing what he saw. No one on either side could believe it! So close! So close!

Then Warroad got a penalty and Greenway-Coleraine got the puck. One of their players went charging down the ice, shot and set the puck behind Billy Poole, as cleanly as a Green Beret sharpshooter bull's-eyes a target. The Greenway-Coleraine fans were feeling the Second Coming: the Warroad fans felt the Four Horsemen of the Apocalypse trampling their dream into dust.

The run for State was over. One minute the Warriors had a foot in the bus door, the next minute the door had slammed, leaving them behind.

This was Henry's first experience with just how fast a sudden-death loss can happen. He learned the stark reality that nothing could be done to recoup the loss. The tragedy was as irrevocable as Humpty Dumpty's fall and nothing could put it together again, no matter how many times he replayed the game in his mind. The stunned Warriors sat in the Roseau locker room teary-eyed again. This was a frustrating end to a year that held so much promise...another year that should have been.

Henry Boucha did not go unnoticed in season play. Region 8 fans were buzzing about him and on the state level rumors were circulating about the unusual hockey prowess of the 9th grade Ojibway Indian boy from Warroad who had risen, and risen shining brightly, on the hockey horizon.

another goodbye

John Hopkins had led the team through an incredible season. Detroit Lakes had offered him a job at a larger salary. He asked the Warroad superintendent for a raise. The issue was taken up and John's request was denied, probably because Dick Roberts was willing to take his place as hockey coach and the "quarterbacks" could work better with him. The Hansons, who had a son on the team and were very happy with the way Hopkins ran the team, felt John had been run out of town and wrote a letter to the Warroad paper complaining about the loss of John Hopkins. John appreciated their concern but it was not the case. John could have stayed at the same salary but he felt he was worth more. Henry came out of his freshman year enriched by John Hopkins. John went on to Detroit Lakes.

14

A team divided

The fall of 1966, Henry's sophomore year and the year of *Star Trek's* inaugural season, hockey swung into place with his Bantam coach, Dick Roberts, as the high school hockey coach and Dale Telle, from Grand Forks, as assistant coach. Telle had seen Henry the year before when the Warriors played in North Dakota against Grand Forks Central. During that game everyone was agreeing that 9th grader, Henry Boucha, was the best player on the ice.

Henry was on defense that year because Roberts felt that way he could play most of the game. There was an excitement to this team. It was the same nucleus that had done so well as Pee-wees, beating Edina, the wealthy suburb of Minneapolis, in the State Bantam Championship. There was fervor about Henry and the media attention he was drawing statewide. Again the little town gathered its hopes but, from the onset, it was clear that the camaraderie was not there. The boys were diverse and always arguing. Part of the team wanted others kicked off the team. There was friction at every juncture. Jealousy surfaced that Henry, a sophomore, was getting so much ice time and attention. The team itself was flat; there was no electricity.

But that didn't stop Alice from going to the games. She just loved watching Henry and was his best fan. She would yell and really get into the action. Having a hero for a son was a welcome respite from her life that had become mundane and saddened from horrifying deaths and involuntary economic upheaval. Alice rode in the car on the many long out of town trips with Coach Roberts' wife. Usually, when Mrs. Roberts complimented her on Henry's playing, she would modestly say he had missed the net and should have scored more, or that he could have played better, but sometimes she would just beam and say, "He sure did!"

At Christmas time the Warroad Warriors were invited to play in a tournament in Coleraine, an iron range town in northeastern Minnesota. They played against one of the premier hockey players to come out of the range, an idol in his own right, Mike Antonovich. Mike later went on to play with the St. Paul Saints and the Minnesota North Stars. Years later, when Antonovich was interviewed on tv during a Minnesota State High School Tournament, he said that Henry was the best player he'd ever played against.

Henry got recognition from the Press at this tournament, which made some of the other parents and players angry. He attracted more attention to himself by wearing little chains through the eyes of his skates. The tournament was the high point of the year for Henry, who ate up the attention he was getting from the press.

The fans were eagerly watching this smooth skating sophomore sensation from the north who could explode up the ice and put their hearts in their mouths. They were fascinated by his three-sixties. They loved his hot-rodding. They were turned on by his blazing forehand and backhand shots. He was just a treat to watch and the fact that he was Indian fascinated them even more.

Like a dud firecracker that wouldn't light, the Warroad Warriors never ignited that year and lost early in the playoffs. This time the loss didn't affect Henry as much, but he learned the value of team unity: if the team was divided it not only weakened the team...the team conquered itself before the opponent even got to them.

Henry was selected to the Minnesota All-State team as a sophomore and he was the first tenth grader to ever receive this honor. His parent's pocketbook couldn't afford the trip to St. Paul to the awards banquet and presentations, so Coach Roberts drove him the long hours south for the ceremony to receive his plaque and patch. Henry was so shy and scared that he didn't say one word to anyone, but it was this event that really started him dreaming about playing in the State Tournament. He wanted to show his skills to the thousands of hockey fans that went to the games.

15

Yearning

Henry's junior year followed the rebellious *Summer of Love:* the antiwar movement that proposed "making love not war." *Bonnie and Clyde* and *The Graduate* were the big movies; *Rolling Stone* made its debut. That fall, on the football field, Henry scored fifteen touchdowns and received accolades in that sport's corner. In hockey he was standout player, heralded throughout the state. He was fabled for streaking down the ice, his smooth style, his searing shot, his intelligent play and brilliant passes.

The jealousy of last year was intensifying. There was name-calling and stabbing behind his back. Coach Roberts, who was very perceptive about what was going on with his team, and who did not want a repeat of last season, took the team down to the other end of the rink out of earshot of the parents, who had gathered to watch practice. He told them how lucky they were to be playing with a kid as good as Henry and told them they should be proud to be playing with him. He told them they all had to get along if they wanted to win; teams who did not respect each other did not win championships. It didn't totally stop the problem but it laid it out in no uncertain terms that Roberts knew what was going on and where he stood on the issue.

Henry got recognition at the Coleraine Tournament again but he yearned to go to the State Tournament. He kept up his incessant skating and practicing on the river. In his skating he was a perfectionist. In his game, he had an uncanny sense of knowing what the play was going to be before it happened.

The Warriors did not make it to the State Tournament again. It was hard for Henry to see other players, like Tim Sheehy of International Falls, whose teams had made it to State, get their names in the paper. He ached to see his name splashed all over the city newspapers of Minneapolis and St. Paul. Again he was selected to the All-State team. This time he was driven to Thief River Falls and boarded the night train to St. Paul. He met Kent LaMoine, from Thief River Falls, who was also going to the banquet for All-State honors. Henry knew more people this year, but it was still a painfully shy experience.

In the spring Henry's thoughts turned to baseball, where he also excelled. It was Tony Stukel, the high school baseball coach's turn to sing his praises. Henry was reliable as well as versatile: he could pitch and play outfield. Henry Boucha was a well-rounded athlete. He could play anything and play it well.

16

In the spring of 1968 the Czechs made a run for freedom from Communist rule...and lost. The Vietnam War, with 550,000 troops committed from the U.S., was escalating to its peak all through 1968 and 1969. Parallel to that, anger was raging among the citizens at home, who realized the senselessness of the war. The summer had seen 10,000 people demonstrate, and be cut down, by the Chicago police at the Democratic National Convention.

Against his country's violent background, Henry, now a high school senior, was quietly dominating high school athletics. As the star football fullback, baseball pitcher and premier hockey player, he had become a hero to the town that was in awe of him.

The gap had widened between Henry and the other players; he was head and shoulders above them. Dick Roberts reported, "(Henry) had the grace of skating that I have never seen in a hockey player. He was very smooth, skated effortlessly -- had tremendous endurance. His vision of the ice was unique, he could see the play developing before the others, so (he) was always in the right place at the right time. Tell him what you wanted him to do and you would get a nod of his head and verbal O.K."

For four years the Warriors had lost their main goal of getting to State. Henry was left with only frustration. He wanted to play at the tournament, and he wanted press coverage for his play at the tournament. His team had to play there to receive that.

Now, of his friends, only he and Rod Estling were left as seniors. They were named co-captains of the Warroad Warriors. The jealous, disgruntled troublemakers had also graduated and what was left was a happy, dedicated, hard working, hungry group of dynamic hockey players. The new team included Frank Krahn, Leo Marshall, Lyle Kvarnlov, Mike Marvin, Ed Huerd, John Taylor, Robert Storey, Jerry Hodgson, Richard Ellerbush, Mike Hanson, Allan Hangsleben (who went on to NHL fame), Mike Stukel and goalie Jeff Hallet. Henry's little brother Eddie was a back-up goalie. They were a great supporting cast to their undisputed star and determined fireballs, uncluttered about life...and living to win.

Early in the season Dick Roberts took Henry aside and told him he set an example for the others. There was something urgent in his voice that caught Henry's attention.

At the beginning of the season the team was resembling a hockey foosball game with the players, except Henry, standing nearly stationary. Henry would take the puck and start down ice, flying after a few strides. When he got blocked he would pass the puck to one of Warroad's standing players, get by the offender, and then his teammate would pass it back to him...the puck went zipping back and forth like a board game.

In Baudette, played on outdoor ice, the players -- as all players from all teams did -- were out to stop the mighty Boucha. Frank Krahn remembers one incredible situation where Henry was flying down the ice near the boards. Every player from Baudette was taking a run at Henry. As Henry would deke them out, each player went splatting against the boards. Henry made it all the way, untouched, for the goal! As the year progressed so did the other Warroad players. They were forming a strong constellation around their star, Henry.

Henry liked to hide behind the net and use it as a decoy, just as he had used the reeds around Government Island as shields when he was a kid. He knew he could beat four guys on open ice, so he'd "sit" behind the net with the puck until one of the opposing players would come in for him. Then he'd take off, jet-propelled, up ice with one player behind him. (His start-up speed from zero to wide open was incredible.) Then he'd fly up ice as the opponents gave their best effort to shut him down.

Henry's shot was so hard he bent a goal pipe in Eveleth. During a game in Thief River Falls he wound up and hit a puck; it sailed above the net and rocketed under the scoreboard...right through the walls of the back end of the rink. In the same game Ronnie Runger skated in the path of one of Henry's shots and got hit in the shin so hard it took his legs out from under him and took him out of the game.

Johnny Mayasich, of Eveleth, had been the Minnesota golden superstar in the early '50's. He broke all the high school records and was a hockey All-American for three college years. Stars had come and gone: no one rivaled Mayasich's fame. But, now the legend of Henry Boucha was growing. He was strong as Hercules to go into the boards with. He was as fast as a cheetah. He was slicker than a Philadelphia lawyer. His shot was faster than a speeding bullet. His abilities were next to Jedi. The fans marveled over this fireball's beautiful skating. Henry was the man. Much to the Faithful's delight, Minnesota hockey's *Second Coming* was here! (People have tried to compare these two luminaries but it is not possible, as they skated in different eras.)

The team was doing well all year but it was a toss-up between Roseau and Warroad in region playoffs. Of the top-rated players in the state Earl Anderson, of Roseau, was rated #3; Henry was ranked #1.

***

hold this thought for later

When Earl Anderson was playing for the Detroit Red Wings he played against the Boston Bruins. Earl was just standing there waiting for play to start when Dave Forbes -- with no warning and completely out of the blue – sucker-punched him flat in the face, resulting in two black eyes.

***

Another tough, serious player was Roseau's Dale Smedsmo. Dale was considered a big jerk to play against but the nicest guy in the world off-ice. Dale had gotten into some problems and had a probation officer who decided to punish Dale by not letting him play high school hockey games. This was a mean-spirited thing to do to a youngster who needed a positive influence to straighten himself out. Frank Macioch, Roseau's new head coach, and several teachers recognized this fact, and knew Dale needed his hockey, where he excelled, to get back on the right track with his life. These brave souls lobbied for him, and he was finally allowed to play varsity the last half of the season.

Dale prevailed and straightened himself out through hockey, which saved his life. He went on to play nine years in the pros, including the NHL Maple Leafs, all because of a few astute teachers and coach who knew Dale was a worthwhile individual and were willing to put their necks on the block for him.

Earl and Dale did not take Henry lightly. They watched him freewheeling around the ice and always wanted him chased down. They hated him when they played him but, at the same time, were in awe of him. They called him "that Indian kid from Warroad," but it was with highest admiration. They just wanted to beat this phenomenon who was so much better than anybody else. Playing against Henry was just a deal and they got extra pumped up playing against him. Every hockey player in the state felt the same way. *Stop Boucha. Make a name for yourself.* Henry was the prime target all year, no matter who they played.

Macioch, put Darrell Foss, a fearless, blue collar hockey player, against Henry all year and said to him, "Stay with

Henry no matter what. If Henry goes to get a hot dog and a Coke, buy it for him!"

Darrell Foss, who waged an admirable campaign against Henry, said Henry was "...hard to contain. Every time he touched the puck it was a threat." He went on to say that, "Henry was a man against boys with a maturity level of a twenty-five-year-old. He was reserved...almost stoic on ice." Foss also noted that Henry controlled the tempo of the game. "There was no question," Foss recalled, " that Henry was the best player ever on the high school level."

The Warroad Warriors and the Roseau Rams had split their two season games. Roseau was fired up to do everything they could to stop Warroad from going to State as Region 8 champs. Darrell Foss stayed on Henry and managed to throttle him down. The goalie, Mike Kvarnlov, Lyle Kvarnlov's cousin, felt fear every time Henry got the puck and electrified the crowd. He was well aware of Henry's crack-of-the-whip, spiffy clean, acura-shot and the force behind it. He knew what he faced with Henry's special skill in being resourceful at getting the puck into the net. Mike Kvarnlov held the net defiantly. He wanted to go to State, and no one was going to score on him. He let one of Henry's in and that was it. No more were going to pass him. Dale Smedsmo, Earl Anderson, Mike Kvarnlov, John Harris (of golf fame) and his younger brother, Robbie (both played hockey for the University of Minnesota) and Gary Ross were all zeroed in on stopping Henry...stopping Warroad. They held their concentration.

In the third period Henry got cut in the head. Dale Telle took him down to the dressing room to get stitched up. Then Henry's defensive partner, Alan Hangsleben, got hurt and, as they were both being attended to, Roseau took the lead 2-1. Roseau put everything they had into stopping Warroad from scoring...and Henry and his band lost the game 2-1 in a great defensive battle.

With whoops and hollars, the Roseau team headed to the center of the ice for a pile and a celebration. The Warroad fans, who had brought clappers to cheer on their team, showered the Roseau Rams with them. The Warriors were devastated by the loss and headed hangdog for the locker room which had been a mourning room for Warroad on previous occasions. Now it served that purpose again. There were tears. There was anguish. They felt they were a better team and somehow they had muffed it.

No one said a word all the way home, but they knew they had one more chance to go in through the back door by becoming Region 3 champs.

Eveleth

In the locker room before the game against Eveleth, played in Hibbing, Henry knew this would be his last high school game if Warroad didn't win. He also knew he would never get to play in the State High School Tournament if his Warriors lost. He was tired of being in second place and weary of going to the banquet in St. Paul, but not taking his equipment with him and having the thrill of skating. All his work for his goal would be vanished.

The game between Eveleth and Warroad was fast paced...the European kind of hockey game that Henry really liked to play in; there wasn't much hitting to slow it down. It was the kind of game where the puck would be lying in the crease but Henry couldn't get at it. It was a game of *sweet* Henry passes to his teammates who launched crowd-pleasing, pretty shots ...but the Eveleth goalie was stopping most of them cold.

Near the end of the second period, with the score tied 2-2, Henry did one of his three-sixty specials with the puck to get around an Eveleth player; this was one of the moves that set his fans' teeth on edge and put their hearts in their mouths. The boy threw his stick back after he was out of it, hitting Henry. The stick sliced Henry's forehead. It was a clean cut and a deep one, and left a fifteen-foot trail of blood behind Henry as he glided to the bench.

The hockey souls fled the bodies of the Warroad fans. All their hopes and dreams to get to State were riding on Henry, their superstar, and his cast of fast-rising stars. The Eveleth fans perked up. Here, finally, was their chance.

In the medical room, the trainer from Hibbing said Henry had to go to the hospital to get it stitched. It was a deep three-inch gash that would need at least twenty stitches. Roberts was frantic. He needed his super-Warrior, his headliner, his mainstay. They had to win this game. There had been so many disappointments in these last years.

A doctor from Hibbing, feeling his services might be needed, came to look at the wound. He told Roberts he could butterfly it shut so Henry could play the rest of the game, and have it stitched up immediately after the game.

The eye had swollen completely shut in a matter of minutes. While Henry was being bandaged, a mighty roar went up in the arena. Eveleth was giving it all they had with Henry gone; Henry had not been off the ice the entire game and they wanted to make hay while their sun shone. The first roar of the fans was followed by another. An Eveleth player had the puck and was racing toward Warroad's goalie, Hallet, and his net. Mike Marvin, in a single Herculean lunge, managed to stop Eveleth. In the biggest play of his life, he kept Warroad in the game.

As the players were getting ready for the face-off, Roberts opened the players' bench door and called to Mike Marvin. Marvin skated over. "What's wrong, Coach?" Marvin asked. "Nothing," Roberts whispered in his ear. "I'm trying to buy time." Then he called Hallet over and adjusted his pads (which, of course, didn't need adjusting). Fans were yelling, "He's stalling!" It worked. As Roberts adjusted the last buckle, Henry came out and was back into the game with one good eye and a heap of determination.

The contest continued its thrill-a-minute pace. The third period was scoreless. The first overtime was scoreless. Everyone was scrambling and shooting, and fans were screaming, but the puck refused to go into the net. Eveleth's star, Doug Palazzari, was giving it all he had. Hallet's mother was pacing behind the stands. The boys were sweating, the jerseys were hot. They were not used to the artificial ice and a warmer building.

Then, with two seconds left on the clock in the second overtime, Henry got a pass from Frank Krahn. He heard someone yell "SHOOT!" With the Ojibway drums beating strong in his heart, Henry let go a hard wrist shot from the top of the circle. It gyroed toward and into the net. The red light went on as the goal judge hit the light. Henry looked at the clock. There was no time left on it – he had scored from a quick-thinking, quick pass from Krahn with a second on the clock...a split-second slower, the goal wouldn't have counted.

This game had pushed Henry's endurance to play until he was exhausted and felt he couldn't push anymore. He had been on the ice every minute except the two-and-a-half minutes it took to get the bandage on him. He loved the feeling of the second wind kicking in after he'd felt he'd spent absolutely everything he'd had...and that was the kind of game that this was.

Their teammates whisked Henry and Krahn up on their shoulders and paraded them around the Hibbing ice. Henry was going to the big Minnesota show and his heart was soaring like the eagles that lived high in the white pine trees off the shores of Buffalo Bay.

In the stands, his parents were allowed the joy of seeing their son on his way to his dream, the State Hockey Tournament.

Little Warroad was going with a team that had gotten

progressively better all year. The camaraderie was there. The electricity was there. Henry was the biggest, brightest star, but like sun dogs, glowing on each side of the sun, his teammates had hung in there; they had learned from him and now they were glowing on their own. The tears in the locker room were those of sheer joy.

Roberts told the superintendent, Stewart Blackorby, that the hockey team would stay in a hotel in Hibbing that night. The next day Ed Strieff, the bus driver, who had been the same driver for all five years of Henry's high school career, drove the stiff school bus seventy miles an hour to get home. He had had it. He had driven the bus south to Bemidji twice, then east to Hibbing...in three days. It was time to get home to his wife.

***

The next few days, before "State," the whole little town was estatic. Everyone who could was making plans for the south-bound pilgrimage to cheer their Warriors on. Jeff Hallet's father shut down his milk delivery business until the tournament was over. Alice and George made plans to go to the games. Those in town who couldn't make it to "the cities," went to International Falls to watch the event on tv.

A tv crew came from Minneapolis to interview Henry and film the team inside the "old barn," but it was too dark in the arena so the team had to tromp outside. At the town sendoff for the team someone yelled, "Speech, Henry, speech!" Henry reddened and looked down.

The town was hopping with excitement. They were so proud. It finally happened. The dream had been realized. Five years of hoping, playing, disappointments, practicing, wishing, and working, had finally ended in gaining a coveted slot at the State High School Hockey Tournament.

They were there because of a magical Indian called Henry, who was part of their heritage, and everyone knew who he was.

17

Into the Fray

There was no lack of media coverage for Henry this year. The Twin Cities Press went wild, plastering his name over every newspaper, going on... "Henry Boucha is coming to town..." "Boucha is great." "Everything they say about the fabulous Henry Boucha is true." "He can be at full speed in two strides." "...the phenomenal senior defenseman..." "Boucha is an excellent skater, with a beautiful, effortless, flowing stride." "Its got an Indian named Henry Boucha who should be playing with the Russians. He can do it all." "...with ace, Henry Boucha." ...

...and on! "He'll be worth a million." "The best hockey player in the state by far is an Indian boy, Henry Boucha, who plays for Warroad High School. He can play anywhere, center, defense or wing and do it all." "Henry Boucha is most prominent." "It's a treat to see him perform." "#1 Warrior." "He is a natural."

...and on! "Warroad superstar Henry Boucha..." "He reminds me of all the great players wrapped into one." "Fans are hanging over the screen to see Boucha." "...he is the best ever." "The boy has a fine future in front of him." "Boucha, the finest athlete." "Gifted youngster." "It's quite a feat when a high school athlete can electrify sports enthusiasts the way Henry Boucha did..." "There's no one like Henry." "Boucha, the incomparable senior."

Henry received a plaque from his Hibbing fans that said, "To Henry Boucha, Minnesota's greatest hockey player." -- Quotes Henry generated in Minnesota newspapers.

"What position would Boucha, the standout defenseman and wing, play at Minnesota? Like the 400 pound gorilla..." Glen Sonmor, University of Minnesota coach cracked, "...any place he wants to."

On a personal level, Henry and his roommate, Ron Estling, were taking in the sights. They were amazed at the traffic, the store windows, the hordes of people and the ten-story hotel. The elevator was a particular fascination...they rode the elevator: up and down, up and down... This year Henry attended the hockey banquet and felt part of the group. His bag was with him and he was ready to play the game. By the time he and Rod checked into bed that first night, they were so hyped-up they couldn't get to sleep, and Coach Roberts got them up early the next morning.

WCCO-TV interviewed Leo Marshall, Frank Krahn and Lyle Kvarnlov who were absolutely struck dumb by the dazzling offices. When they got on tv the interviewer was asking them questions that were to be answered by explanatory sentences.

Interviewer: "How do you like it here?"
Warroad Player: "O.K."
Interviewer: "How are the rinks?"
Warroad Player: "Fine."
Interviewer: "What is it like playing against your cousin?"
Warroad Player: "Fun."
Interviewer: "It seems as if you are the Cinderella team at this tournament?"
Warroad Player: "Yup."

Dick Roberts was standing behind the cameras frantically using hand gestures to relay to the star-struck boys to expand on their monosyllabic answers. They never did.

Southwest

1969 was the first time a State Tournament game had been played at the Met Center, home of the NHL North Stars team. It was a huge place. The ice sheet was enormous. The nets seemed bigger to the goalies. The artificial ice was slower than the ice they were used to. There was a mammoth scoreboard with four sides hanging from the roof of the arena. Seats for the fans extended skyward. The building was warm, lungs were tight and equipment felt heavier. The kids were overwhelmed by the awesomeness of it all. Henry felt little and had jitters.

Their first game was against Southwest, a huge Minneapolis school with their fabulous goalie, Brad Shelstad. At the start of the game Lyle Kvarnlov got the puck and dumped it! He couldn't move. The game seemed immaterial to the surroundings: surreal. The swells of people cheering...the odd ice... Everything flowed around them, but it was like they weren't there. Early in the game the team sensed, that by the cheering of the crowd when Warroad did something exciting, the crowd was behind them. But the stage-struck, underdog Warriors fell behind Southwest 2-0 early in the game.

Henry had a way to bounce the puck off the boards, turn around the opposite direction (a one-eighty) and go down the ice, leaving his pursuer still looking at the boards wondering where Henry was. He did this early in the game against Southwest, then went screaming down center ice on a rush, as the fans were yelling, and let go, firing a blistering backhand shot (as the fans were going bonkers). He hit the cross bar! The noise from the crowd sounded like a fifty-floor building being demolished.

It is rumored that a North Stars' player, who was just as

pumped as the rest of the crowd, exclaimed that Henry's backhand was better than any of the Minnesota North Stars.

When it was over the Warriors outshot Southwest by eleven and won the game 4-2. Henry had an assist and a score. The other Warroad players rose to the occasion: they had learned well from playing with Henry. This was no longer a one man team.

After the Southwest game, Lyle took his skates off in the locker room. The reporters were anxious to interview Henry and Lyle on tv on the ice: Henry because he was the sensation – Lyle because he had scored two goals. Henry yelled "Lyle, we're on tv!" Lyle ran out on the ice with his socks on. The man with the mike said to Henry, "You had a great game." Henry replied, "No, it was done by the other guys." Lyle marveled at this. Henry <u>had</u> had a great game. He was all over the ice wowing the fans and yet he was giving the other guys the credit...and he meant it!

The interview was over, the Zamboni was whirring toward them and Henry skated off the ice. Lyle was left on the ice with his socks stuck on it. The Zamboni was bearing down on him. Henry was yelling, "Come on, we've got to get out of here," then realizing his teammate was in trouble, Henry raced back to help Lyle unstick his socks.

Roseau

Henry and his roommate, Rodney, didn't sleep well that night but again Roberts got them up early the next morning. Henry was followed by sportswriters and fans, and enjoyed the attention and seeing his name in the paper as any athlete does.

Warroad had to face their archrival, Roseau, for the second tournament game. Both teams were tired with the handicaps of little rest and being a long way from home, but the rivalry was hot and it would be a battle. Coach Macioch's game plan was to box Henry in. Macioch knew his hockey. He had played on the first state tournament game in 1945 and been the assistant coach in Roseau under Almquist for twelve years. The crowd was wild. Everyone was there to see Henry. Roseau was ahead 2-1. Foss, the shadow, who had grown very proficient at keeping Henry tied up, ended up in the penalty box. Macioch knew it was a bad call and he had to watch as a freed-up Henry scored to tie the game. Henry tallied an assist and an unassisted goal that night to keep his screaming, adoring fans happy, and Warroad "trimmed the Rams" 3-2 to send them on to the Minnesota State High School Championship game.

18

Hype

The Minnesota State High School Championship games have always had a build-up to them. There is a buzz-current of excitement, with the media front and center touting the players who they, the sportswriters, have targeted as being the best and the players who they, the reporters, have followed and written about over the years that lead up to the tournament.

But no one had seen anything like the hoopla preceding the 1969 championship game. Not only was Henry a hockey sensation, he was Indian and that fact took over the fancy of the Minnesota crowd. Somewhere in the mix from the 1950's to the late 1960's the belittlement-of-Indians of ten years earlier had been replaced. Minnesotans were truly proud to have an American Indian sports achiever -- and one of such magnitude was more than they had asked for. Henry was lavished with attention. He was talked about in every nook and cranny of Minnesota.

This incredible phenomena of wanting a Native American to do well, and then having Henry fit the bill *so utterly amazingly,* took on a personality of its own. It turned into the granddaddy of hype, which gave birth to a single-minded crowd with momentum and character, which grew into the force of a tsunami wave.

***

Obscure little faraway Warroad, with its romantic bigger-than-life American Indian hero who could wow the crowds like no one ever had before, was the Cinderella team. Warroad's opponents, the larger-than-life wealthy suburb Edina, even though it had never won a state high school hockey championship, was proclaimed Goliath.

19

Game of games

Henry skated onto the bright ice-stage of the 1969 Minnesota State High School Championship game to the tumultuous welcome of almost 15,000 fans. The roars of happy spring thunders echoed throughout the arena. He teased the crowd with his warm-up, sending shivers like the running lights of Las Vegas, up and down their spines. His coaches stood proud and tall. Alice, George, Shirley, Jim, and David, who had just gotten married, sat excitedly watching his virtuoso performance as the thunder clapped around them.

The hoopla quieted down, while the Edina band played the Star Spangled Banner, but the hearts inside the fans and players didn't. The strains faded, the mad cheering resumed. It was time to play hockey.

period 1

To his radio fans in the north, Bernie Bergraff, of Roseau's radio station KRWB said to his microphone, "Well, let's fasten our seat belts." The fans needed them. In the first twenty-two seconds of the game, the first shift, Edina's Rick Fretland scored -- drilling one high in the upper right corner of Jeff Hallet's net.

Edina, coached by Willard Ikola, was favored because of its depth; they had three solid lines. Warroad did not have many horses on defense but they were excellent forecheckers. But the crowd wasn't there to see Edina -- they were there to see Henry and every time Henry carried the puck the crowd-wave swelled: cheering, screaming, for him.

Then Steve Curry, an Edina defenseman, took a full puck to his upper lip, which added some tension to the Edina fans and put him out of action while he was being stitched up.

During the game there was no doubt about it, Henry was in control...always rushing, passing and shooting. Edina's goalie, enthusiastic and determined Doug Hastings, kept Edina in the game. He was saving Henry's shots...or they were clearing the side of the net by a hair or sailing above the goal like a barn swallow. The volume of the crowd went up and down, like a wave on the ocean, behind the shots.

Warroad's Hangsleben got control of the puck. He took his time, refusing to be rushed, and sent it to Kvarnlov who managed to get open. Kvarnlov, in turn, took his time getting the puck to Leo Marshall, who was in good scoring position. Leo didn't panic. He calculated and shot the puck, which landed behind Hastings. Before the puck settled, the volume in the Met Center rose full throttle, with the crowd's roar spilling down onto the ice. The score was 1-1. For the moment the crowd could live with that. Henry would score for them; they wanted to savor watching him play and shoot and skate.

Henry got a golden opportunity and let off with a blazing backhand which cometed toward Hastings and his Edina net. The volume of the screaming fans went with it. Hastings watched it streaking toward him and his net like a heat-seeking missile. He reached out and grabbed it out of the air! The crowd was wild. How could Hastings do that? The play didn't let up. Henry slid one to Warrior Richard Ellerbush, who got it to Eddie Huerd who banged it toward the net.... Yes! The puck went past Hastings. Warroad scored...and their hero had a hand in it. The goal brought the house down and the big board lit up 2-1 with the 2 in the Warroad column.

Warroad always forechecked tenaciously and tightly in the Warroad zone. It was part of their game. They were doing it that night, remembering everything Coach Roberts had taught them and doing it textbook style.

Henry grabbed the puck on his stick and rushed it down the ice *oooooooooooooohhhhhhhhhhhhing* the crowd. He wound up, had Hastings beat, and let go a blistering shot that took the fans out of their seats. Bing! The puck hit the pipe! The crowd orchestrated a moan. He snatched the rebound, as two Edina players practically hung on him, and took a long shot and missed...by a hair...again. The crowd was going nuts.

Back at his microphone, Bernie Bergraff was duly reporting this back to the northern audience.

The puck bounced off the boards. Henry got control and shot again...with the pesky Edina players glued to him. It hit Edina's Bruce Carlson, then an Edina player got control. Henry stole it from him and shot again. The puck whizzed by the net, missing it by a duck feather!

Buzzer. End first period.

The scoreboard stayed the same, 2-1, in favor of Warroad. The play had been breathtaking. Their Henry had blown through their souls as fresh and exhilarating as a Pacific storm and it was a feel-good crowd that exited the stands for refreshments.

During the first intermission, Bernie entertained his northern listeners with interviews. The first was Al Mackie, a former

Warroad coach, who was coaching in Farmington, Minnesota. The second was John Gilbert, writer for the *Minneapolis Star*.

Mackie said, "Boucha knows how to pace himself. (He) won't tire as fast as people think he will. If Warroad can pop another one, the roof will go in on Edina. When Henry was introduced it must have backed up the Edina team off their blue line by two feet. I've never heard anything like it."

Gilbert reported: "Warroad fore-checks like their own goal's on fire. They fore-check into the lobby. Edina never wound up in the first period. Hastings is keeping Edina in the game. No one notices anyone but Henry on the ice..."

hit

The Warroad team came back out on the ice for the second period to another ovation from the adoring fans, but they were soon to be disappointed. At the beginning of the period Edina's Carlson brothers tied the score, then a minute later, with Warroad shorthanded, the Fretland boys scored a go-ahead goal. Henry was checking like crazy. The pace was frenzied. He got off a backhand pass to Kvarnlov, who almost scored. The Warriors, who wanted desperately to tie the game, were pelting Hastings.

Then, halfway through the second period, Henry got the puck and went flying down the ice sheet with a power and beauty of skating never seen or equaled in high school hockey. He was on a mission to score...for his team, his parents (oh how he loved to see his parents smile after all the tragedy and hardships) his fans, and the people back home. He sprinted across the center-line and he streaked down the ice, to the roar of the fans that swelled like a tsunami wave heading toward shore behind him. He was in control of the ice. He was the best player to have ever played in the Minnesota State High School Hockey Tournament. He had won the hearts and the imagination of the fans.

Henry let go with a blistering slap shot from the blue line. The sound from the crowd was deafening as the soundwave headed higher, hovering over the shore. The puck flew like a hard-hit baseball, heading right for the net, and bounced off Hastings. The crowd continued yelling, screaming, cheering, straining as the wave was peaking...Henry chased his rebound into the corner with Edina's medium-height Jim Knutson skating fast and hard on his heels.

Henry was looking down in this split second, digging the puck out and, just as he tried to pick it up on his stick, Knutson caught up with him. SLAM! Henry bounced heavily into the boards as Knutson threw his elbow into his ear. BANG! Henry's head slammed the unforgiving Plexiglas and, as his conscious systems melted down, he sank to the ice.

Behind the montage scene, the crowd silenced for an ever-so-brief moment, taking this in. Then its hush was followed by a deafening crescendo as the soundwave gathered to its crest and stretched, hovering in anger. Then the sound crashed, thundering into furious and angry *boooooooooooooo's* -- as angrily and as furiously as the mighty tsunami crashes upon its shore. Their Indian Brave lay motionless as the screaming of the mob floated above his unconscious body.

When Henry regained consciousness, he had lost his equililibrium. He had no sense of up or down. He felt very sick inside and his head felt as if a Sioux spear had been rammed through it. The crowd was insane, booing Jim Knutson and cheering for Henry at the same time. Bernie Bergraff called the hit "vicious," "malicious" and "uncalled for." Coach Roberts sprinted across the ice. When he got to the scene, Henry moaned, "I'm done." Dick Roberts couldn't believe his ears.

The Edina band piped up a tune. Then everyone was standing and cheering for Henry, trying to envelop him in a noise they thought might help heal him. He was pulled up and dragged off the ice between Coach Roberts and Snapper Stein, the trainer from the University of Minnesota. The great hero had been felled and the crowd felt an agony that the "big one" had been taken from them. George and Alice were paged over the loudspeaker system to report to the First Aid Room. Edina had gone from being merely the threat Goliath into being the hated enemy.

***

Henry was taken to the First Aid Room as everything around him spun like a wild ride at a fair. His jersey was cut off. An ambulance took him to Ramsey Hospital in St. Paul, away from the game where he wanted to be. He was dazed and was in excruciating pain, and the ride to the hospital seemed forever. To make it worse, under it all, he had a terrible sense of letting his team down.

Just like being taken from his little happy home on Buffalo Bay, he was taken from his high school team. He wasn't there for the second half of the second period when Frank Krahn gave it all he had and scored twice from assists from Bob Storey to tie Edina 4-4. He wasn't there when the little Warroad team, with their brightest star gone from their sky, formed a brilliant constellation and fought on to the end. He wasn't there for the overtime. And, he wasn't there when Edina scored the winning goal. He wasn't there when he was named to the All-State team. He wasn't there for the last homage the people of Minnesota wanted to give him, and that he would have liked to have heard.

aftermath

Coach Roberts, who had adopted the denial mode, couldn't believe Henry was not coming back to the game. Henry had always come back when he was hurt. He kept looking for Henry to come skating back onto the ice. When Telle came back from the First Aid Room with the awful news that Henry had been taken away by an ambulance, Roberts still couldn't believe it.

During and after the game, the fans were buzzing with controversy over Jim Knutson's hit. Henry, the *Northern Star*, who was already a legend, was now a fallen star; the Warroad team had battled bravely back; and Edina, who had never won a state high school tournament game, had clinched its first state title. These incredible events would indeed have been enough to satisfy any hockey fan for a very long time.

But, it was not over yet.

At the conclusion of the game, the President of the Board of Control of the Minnesota State High School League, Clair McMann, also principal of St. Paul Johnson High School, said the St. Paul Auditorium was "a dimly lit dusty barn compared to this palace." He was comparing the new Metropolitan Sports Center to the old St. Paul Auditorium. This remark drew the wrath of the St. Paul fans.

Then, when it was time to give Henry's All-State award, McMann said that the next award was going to a member of a minority race and went on to add: "Our ancestors took most of the land away from his ancestors. Let's give a big chunk of it back to him tonight." No one moved on the Warroad bench to come and pick up the award. Finally, Henry's younger brother, Eddie, skated out to pick it up. This comment drew the ire of everyone who felt as Jim Kobluchar later summed, "...it was only a hockey game, not an exercise in collective guilt." McMann, a good man, resigned over the incident.

Someone else said, "Let's pause for a moment of silence for

our fallen hero," and the announcer on WLOL, who was sitting next to Bernie Bergraff, said over the radio that Henry Boucha had died. There were people in the northlands who turned off their radios in shock, thinking Henry was, in fact, dead.

All in all, this multifaceted 1969 Minnesota State High School Championship contest held every ingredient that made it the game of games.

Jim Knutson

Jim Knutson's check became the most famous check in Minnesota hockey history.

Jim Knutson was a boy who got caught up in the hyper-excitement of the game of games. He saw his chance for a hit on the great one and checked his opponent, the mighty Boucha, with definite purpose, force and excitement, but not with malice. There was no gloating or any recognition that he had injured Henry; Knutson skated back into action as a player would after any satisfying hit. The whistle did not blow until Knutson was back at the blue line and the referees realized Henry was seriously hurt. Then Knutson was given a two-minute penalty for elbowing.

Every time Jim Knutson touched the puck for the rest of the game, the throng jeered. They screamed "hatchet man" and "cake eater" over the boards every time he got near them. When Jim Knutson received All-State recognition, the crowd booed.

It is always sad when a hockey player on any level gets hurt; but when the great hero is hurt...and the hero is from the underdog team...the crowd is unforgiving.

Knutson did not have a history of being a dirty player. He went on to play for the University of Minnesota, where he was never involved in controversy, but for years Jim Knutson held the stigma of the one who intentionally took out the great Henry Boucha.

***

The Warriors went home on the bus for the first time in five years without Henry, who stayed behind in the hospital for three days. His inner ear had been injured and the drum had been torn. To repair the damage, the doctors first deadened the inside of his ear with Novocaine delivered by a huge needle attached to a syringe. When it was injected Henry felt like his head would explode. The operation was successful, but when the numbness wore off, Henry had a horrible day with the pain.

Henry got back to Warroad via an ambulance to the Minneapolis airport and then he, Alice and George flew home in Swede Carlson's plane, which had snow skis on it. The plane landed on the Warroad River. That night at the school, there was a huge reception for Henry.

Neither the Minnesota High School league nor Warroad High School carried insurance to pay for Henry's ear surgery. The *St. Paul Pioneer Press* announced that the league didn't pay. Money poured in...more than enough to pay for his hospital expenses. The extra funds were used for his teeth, that were in a sad state, to be repaired. The dentist put in a gold front tooth. Henry loved his gold tooth.

***

Henry had been pretty much a loner during high school. His good friends were Rod Estling and Bob Wentzel. He had plenty of things to deal with in his young life: his parents' grief and economic problems; his status as an adulated sports figure; his own time and effort into sports; and the pressure put on him by the townspeople and coaches. He was so good at what he did! He tried to please a lot of people. He was quiet, a good person, honest and nice. He presented himself apart from the others and also seemed so much older than his peers. Paulette Henke, a physical education teacher, became a person Henry could talk to. They developed a deep friendship. Paulette could see the whole picture clearly, as she was not from Warroad.

The ending of his senior year was terrible. Henry did not get to finish the game of games, which, with Henry's force, could well have had a different outcome. Yet Henry's star shone bright in his final year of high school hockey. This brilliance was so rare, it was assured to shine forever in the hearts of Minnesotans. In 1969 he was the undisputed hero of Minnesota hockey, and the most charismatic ever to come out of the state high school ranks.

Henry was ready for the next step.

PART IV

SILVER

JOIIA... "SILVER"
OJIBWAY

20

Some "bear with it" Olympic history
...for those who want to know

In the winter of 1969, when Henry was *oooooooooohhhhhing*
the Minnesota crowds, the U.S. National Team took a trouncing
in Sweden. This loss placed them in the B group for the 1970
Nationals in Romania the following winter. The question of the
U.S. not sending a representative team to Nationals in Romania
in 1970 and Switzerland in 1971, and Japan for the 1972
Olympics, was seriously considered by the Amateur Hockey
Association, United States (AHAUS).

The U.S., as a whole, was in upheaval. The Vietnam War was
raging; the country was divided about it. Nixon was president.
Manson had performed his grisly murders. A man walked on the
moon. Woodstock "happened," and *Butch Cassidy* was the rage
of the Silver Screen. Eisenhower died and an era passed with
him, and *Big Bird* was born spawning a new era.

On the international scene, Meir was elected Israel's Prime
Minister; Uddafi strong-armed his way to lead Libya; the Beatles
went to India and the Communists controlled the Soviet Bloc.

double standard

At that time, in order to participate in the Olympics, a player
needed to maintain an amateur status. Unfortunately, there
were two sets of standards in the world for what constituted
"amateur." In the set the U.S.A. and other Democratic countries
were members of, "amateur" meant someone who was not
officially a "pro" league player and thus did not bear the label
"professional" player. In the other set, the set made up of the
Soviet Bloc Communist countries, another rule applied. Their
leaders insisted no "pro" leagues existed in the Eastern Bloc and,
therefore, those countries had no "professional" players. *All* the
Communist Bloc players were labeled "amateur," on the
technicality that they did not *call* their teams "pro" or their
players "professional!" The comrades, the Soviets argued poker-
faced, played for their country and were accordingly "amateurs."
It was common knowledge that the Bloc amateurs were parallel
to the professional players of the Democratic countries.

The top players in the Soviet countries were supposedly not
paid as our professional players were *but* they were provided top-
of-the-line living quarters, the highest quality food, the finest

cars, the best medical care, and the fabulous vacations afforded only the most prestigious Soviets. These athletes lived lavishly as folk heroes, plus they were paid a cash allowance. Worse, these men played together for years, sparring with their teams and honing their skills to perfection. The result of this inequity was that amateur boys from Democratic countries who came together for a few months to form a National Team (boys who were aspiring to be pros and skating for the love of it), were pitted against hardcore, professional men.

This situation remained a bone of contention between the smug East and the frustrated West for years. Officials from the cheated western countries bared their teeth as they snarled and threatened the Olympic committee, but were never able to change the bogus rules. Finally an angry Canada, in protest of the partial-to-the-other-guy standard, stopped sending teams to International Competitions, including the '72 and '76 Olympics.

decision

In the summer of 1969, Murray Williamson, former All-American hockey player, was answering AHAUS' questions: should the United States hockey team drop out of the unfair International Competition and not send *boys* into battle against the Soviet, Czech, East German, Finnish and Polish *men*.

In 1972, the Russian Red Army team was at its zenith; the Russians were in their prime.

But this was 1969, and, if a U.S. team were to participate in the 1970 National Games in Romania, they had to be ready to slug their way through the lower B group in the international level, and place on top of that bracket. Then they would be eligible to get back into the A division for the 1971 Nationals in Switzerland, in order to have a shot at the 1972 Olympics.

Most of the AHAUS decision-makers looked at the inequitable situation realistically, and thought taking a team of amateurs to play against Soviet Bloc pros was a losing situation and a waste of money. However, they did not want to rely solely on their own convictions, so they asked Murray Williamson to study the matter.

21

Murray's dream

Murray mulled the situation over carefully, weighing all aspects. He knew the strengths of the U.S.S.R. lie in:

1. The strength and skills of their players.
2. Their rigorous training techniques.
3. The fact that the same players were together over a long period of time.
4. Being able to play highly competitive teams.
5. Tarasov, the Soviet coach, was the greatest hockey mind, ever.

Murray made a blueprint to determine if the problems facing the U.S. National and Olympic teams were solvable. He determined on the first point that a swat team could indeed be put together from U.S. talent. The second point he had to concede was not resolvable this year but could be implemented the following year. The third issue, that of longevity, couldn't be dealt with entirely, but a nucleus of players could be started in 1970, strengthened in 1971, and by the 1972 Olympics, the team would have a cohesiveness. Again, the fourth point was not possible this year, but the following year AHAUS could line up a pre-national schedule of games for the team, which would consist of minor pro teams and college teams. This year, perhaps a few games could be hastily put together so the team could toughen up against some strong teams. The fifth point, that of competing against Tarasov, would be a toughie. Murray was not delusional about a gold medal, but he felt that with a strong American coach the team could be respectable.

Murray's tight, professional and well-thought-out plan on forming a successful U.S. Olympic team three years hence was convincing to AHAUS. They caught his enthusiasm and agreed to back a team with his recommendations, and asked him to coach it. He said he would take the team if it would be a three-year deal. AHAUS agreed.

It was *late* for organizing the 1970 National Team. Murray had only two and a half months to put a team together that could win in the B group. He planned to assemble the best college and amateur players he could gather over Christmas break. They would practice and then reassemble just before Nationals. As Murray's brain spun the wheel of eligible players, Henry Boucha was on the top. The brilliant high school star was young enough to be a three-year nucleus player, and would be instrumental in making Murray's medal dream a reality. Murray faced his three-year program with a Technicolor dream, backed up by a black-and-white strategy. This included the energy and the hard work needed to place the U.S. in the top three teams of the world at the 11th Olympiad in Sapporo, Japan, in 1972.

22

Jets

The first day he was legally able to, in the spring of 1969, amid fanfare and media hype, Henry signed a letter of intent with the University of Minnesota. Glen Sonmor, Minnesota's "Golden Gophers" coach, was licking his chops over the anticipation of the multi-skilled Boucha being part of his team. As one of the hottest high school athletes in the nation, outstanding in hockey, football and baseball, Henry could have gone almost anywhere, and was actively courted by Midwestern and Eastern colleges. Dick Roberts was pleased and proud that Henry had signed with Minnesota's "U" and the case was closed. Roberts was looking forward to watching his star play in Minneapolis next year.

The Canadian Junior A hockey teams wanted Henry also. He was asked play for the Winnipeg Jets, then a junior team. The general manager of a Montreal junior team came to Warroad to talk to Henry and gave him a ticket east. Henry put the ticket on his dresser and never used it.

summer league

That summer, Henry's mind clicked to a new place that caused him to think for himself. It happened because he was invited to play with a group of supposedly cream-of-the-crop Minnesota high school players in a prestigious summer league out of Edina, Minnesota.

John Roberts, Dick Roberts' son, home from West Point, was also in the league. In one of the games, Henry was playing against John. Henry put a move on John; John lost his balance and fell clumsily. As he went down he lost control of his stick, whacking Henry in the mouth with it. Henry lost his beautiful, just refurbished, front teeth. The summer league had insurance and replaced them.

The office was deluged with calls asking when Henry would be playing. His games were always well-attended, but Henry was disappointed in the summer league. It was anti-climatic to the thrilling Warroad high school season, and the summer league players, on the whole, lacked luster. No one put out what they could have. As the ho-hum summer droned on, Henry felt more and more that the league was a waste of time for him. Henry could never stand to play anything unless it was always his best, with the idea of always improving. Henry reasoned the apathy of the summer league was because they weren't playing for a specific goal. Aside from the few standouts scattered throughout the teams, including Wally Olds, Mike Antonovich, Gary Gambucci, and Charlie Brown, the group did not consist of players of the skill level he wanted to be playing with. Henry was unhappy. He was itching to play, to really play with the highest powered competition he could, with the players whose hearts beat to play hockey. He wanted to hone his skills against theirs...to feel the throb of the win and the pain of defeat because you really wanted to win and because you really hated to lose.

Pistol Pete

Meanwhile, in Manitoba, Canada, the Winnipeg Jets' coach, Eddie "Pistol Pete" Dorohoy, was racking his brain on how to lure the multi-talented Boucha to his team. Young Boucha was the *big one* he didn't want to get away. Most eighteen-year-olds, he reasoned, could be bought if the stakes were worth it. In early September he drove to Warroad, in a pink Cadillac convertible, to talk with Henry and to sweeten the pot: a car, an apartment, plus a healthy living allowance. Timing is everything. Dorohoy didn't know it, but this titillating offer couldn't have come to Henry at a better time. Henry sat outside his parents' house and listened to Dorohoy for over three hours. When the conversation was over, Henry had made a decision...his own decision.

Henry knew he wanted to play hockey and play hockey only. He also knew he wanted to play with boys who understood sacrifice as he did, and who were as serious about hockey being #1 in their lives as he was. Studies, he knew, were not on the card in his viewfinder; he didn't want studies *and* hockey. He wanted hockey. His goal in life was to play in the NHL and he knew the quickest and least cluttered way to get there was to play juniors. The Jets were especially attractive because Winnipeg was close: only two hours from Warroad. He wanted to be within striking distance of home. Dorohoy's offer of money and an apartment was juicy bait. Henry felt independent and the thought of being financially free and being able to do what he wanted was impossible to ignore.

a good decision

Henry had grown up over summer. He was separated from Coach Roberts now: by time, by new experiences, by playing with boys less focused than he and by the fact that Roberts was no longer his coach. Without consulting Roberts, or anyone else, for that matter, Henry, always independent as far as his own life was concerned, chomped Dorohoy's bait and signed with the Jets. In doing so, he shocked Roberts and the smug Minnesota hockey world, who felt the way up the ladder of hockey success included a college hockey career (preferably the University of Minnesota) and, that Henry had made a colossal mistake at a young age.

a bad decision

Then, almost immediately, without thinking of the long-term consequences, Henry made plans to marry seventeen-year-old Deborah Bleau. For Henry, marriage was not an illogical move: in the Indian and French communities it was not uncommon to marry young. But he and Debby had slogged through an argumentative, unstable, rocky relationship since eighth grade, and his family and friends knew it was a terrible mistake.

During high school Henry had a mentor-friendship with a first-year high school teacher, Paulette Henke. On a personal level, he should have realized from that, that a normal male-female relationship is comprised of supporting and listening to the other person; that a relationship is not based on immaturity and jealousy. He should have looked at the marriage of Alice and George, his own parents, and realized that a good marriage goes though rough times, and, it is imperative to have a trusting, mature union – one that breeds content. But he didn't.

Since his eighteenth birthday in June, Henry had made two major life decisions: one a very centered and mature career move -- and another, which would prove disastrous. This peaceless union would siphon his energy and focus for four precious years.

Jets

All through his high school years, Henry owned no hockey equipment: the school had provided it. So when he arrived at the St. James Arena in Winnipeg for the Jets tryout, they had to dig around for equipment for Henry. One hundred hopefuls showed up on the ice the first day. Henry didn't know anyone. Dorohoy whittled down the pool, and the team was finally selected after the kids, who were trying out for pro teams and didn't make them, came back. Henry found an apartment for $400.00 a month and returned to Warroad to marry Debby in October after buying a car in Roseau for $400.00 cash.

The Jets were a haven for Henry. It gave him an opportunity to concentrate fully on hockey. The outlaw Western Canada Hockey League was wild, woolly, fun, rambunctious, and a great deal stepped up from the polite hockey he had played in the Braemar summer league, and the relatively tame Minnesota high school league. The rugged players afforded him the opportunity to indeed move up his game. He loved it. Besides Henry, there were five mighty players who all went on to the NHL: Neal Komadowsky, Chris Odelafson and Jimmy Hargraves to the Canucks, Brian Cadle to the Jets, and Wayne Chernicki to the L.A. Kings.

Henry had to learn how to take hard hits and how to play a much rougher game, while still concentrating on his skills. True, Henry had been singled out as a moving target in high school by his peers, but now the whole league was tough, older and much, much, stronger than his high school opposition...plus being recklessly competitive.

The players were dedicated, physical, snarling opponents and were after everyone. Henry had to harden and add serious checking and roughness to his finesse game. The Winnipeg team concept was offensive and defensive zones. Henry learned little tricks, and how to manipulate other players, which would prove invaluable in his career.

Then there was another curious aspect. Henry was out of the U.S. and away from his adoring fans. This was his first exposure to not being the most beloved and revered player on the ice. In fact, the Canadian crowds hated Americans, and were cruel, yelling obscenities about anything to distract him from his game. Being Indian was hurled at Henry as a bad thing to be. He was confused, but, as he sorted it out, he realized the crowds were jibing the other players too. Several times the Jets had to have police escort them out of the arena to protect them from the mobs. Henry's skills increased: he had twenty-five goals before Christmas!

Henry exchanged his glasses for contact lenses, that felt like sandpaper in his eyes. He was constantly losing them and crawling around the ice, trying to find one.

He and Debby fought continually, or, on the rare occasions they weren't fighting, she was bored, so she didn't stay with him in Winnipeg very much. He was alone in his apartment for most of the time. The boy from the big family and the huge extended family hated being alone.

On November 16, 1969, John Gilbert of the *Minneapolis Star* did a piece on Henry for the Sunday picture section. John found Henry to be a well-adjusted hockey player who was enjoying his work. He was learning new things, including junior rules, playing center instead of defense (which included new positioning on the ice for him) knocking more people down, and working very hard to achieve his goal of one day playing in the NHL.

John found out that the Canadians did not think it was odd that Henry had passed up college for junior hockey. In his article John wrote: "With Henry's talent," Dorohoy said, "it's natural that he should come to Canada where he will get the ice time and the type of competition he needs."

In Bismarck, for a game there, Bill Yonchuk, the Jets trainer from Estevan, saw Henry walk by a bar he was in. He motioned the eighteen-year-old Henry inside and poured him a beer, which turned into a few glasses. Henry was feeling chipper and ended up drinking five or six pitchers of beer. Tuned up, he ordered a pepperoni pizza and got very sick. The worst of it was, he had a game in a few hours. He surprisingly played "pretty good" -- the first half -- before his legs gave out.

The Jets went on a long road trip. First they traveled to Brandon, to play the Wheat Kings; then on to Estevan, to spar with the Bruins; next it was up to Saskatoon, on the lonely plains of Saskatchewan, for a match with the Blades; then on to Swift Currant, to go against the Broncos. They trekked west to Calgary, Alberta, to test the Centennials, then straight up north to Edmonton, to battle the Oil Kings. Henry loved the camaraderie of the bus trips. The guys would sleep on the bus, play *hearts*, and talk. It was fun staying in the motels along the way. One night they were running up and down the halls having a water fight. Henry opened a door to throw water in on a kid, who slammed the door on Henry's hand and the glass. Henry was badly cut; his hand and fingers were laid open. He had go to the hospital to be stitched up. He didn't want the coach to know, so some of his buddies took him in. In Saskatoon there was a brawl and Henry couldn't fight because of his hand.

The Jets lost every game on that trip and were on a seven game losing streak. Dorohoy was going wild. At the end of the trip, he got fired, and Henry didn't see him again that season. Nick Michkowski, a former New York Rangers player, took over.

Then, in December, another decision faced teenage Henry. Murray Williamson caught up with him. Henry had bruised ribs (possibly a cracked rib) and was playing shot up with Novocaine. He did not feel he had played a good game under the circumstances. Murray asked Henry how he felt he played and Henry explained about the ribs. Murray asked him to try out for the 1970 U.S. National Team that would be playing in Romania in the International Tournament in February. Murray was watching Henry with his ever-eagle eye. He knew Henry was maturing playing with the juniors instead of college and would be an even stronger competitor than he had at first bargained for.

Henry had another dream aside from playing in the NHL, and that was to represent his country in the Olympics. This team would be the first step toward that goal. Ever since the Christian brothers of Warroad had played on the 1960 Olympic team, it had been a dream of Henry's to play for the "Red, White and Blue." He knew the caliber of players on the National Team would be even more competitive than the Jets. Henry was not concerned about falling behind his Junior A cohorts but looking forward to what he could learn from the older, more experienced players.

The Jets didn't want to let Henry go, but in the end Murray Williamson yanked some chains and the management was persuaded.

Henry was to be gone from the Jets three weeks with the National Team: the last two weeks of February and the first week of March. The National Team would also play four exhibition games before they left for Romania. When he got back from Romania he would join the Jets for the last three weeks of their season. By the time Henry would join the National Team, the legend from Warroad had as many games as two full seasons of college play.

Hockey was going well; his personal life was not. When he joined the other players to try out for the National Team, in Bloomington, Minnesota, he and Debby were same-old-same-old: fighting constantly. He was coming home tired from the tryouts but Debby would not let him sleep; he was getting one to two hours sleep a night. Henry was exhausted and was afraid he would not make the team but didn't say anything to Murray. Driving back to Warroad from the Twin Cities, he thought he wouldn't make it and kept drifting off. When he and Debby did get back home, he went to bed and slept for sixteen hours. The marriage was far from his parents' quiet, peace-filled years on Buffalo Bay. There was no companionship, only a bickering existence ridden with jealousy and immaturity.

23

the gathering

When the National tryouts were held, the contestants were a veritable feast of All-Americans, heavy-hitters and big names in U.S. hockey. Henry was the youngest player trying out.

Henry met Ozzie O'Neill, who would become his best friend on the team, at the tryout and they struck it off from the beginning. Ozzie, from Marquette, Michigan, was playing with the USHL in Marquette. Not in college nor an All-American, Ozzie was nonetheless a tenacious player, and determined to make this National Team. Murray wanted the best he could get and to his credit, titles were not the only qualification for making his team. The first time Henry and Ozzie met, Henry shook Ozzie's hand and commented that Ozzie looked like someone in Warroad.

One week after Christmas the unfinalized, but trimmed down pool, of wanna-be National Team players, had games scheduled against the University of North Dakota and the University of Minnesota. They lost the first game 2-1 against North Dakota at the Bismarck, North Dakota Civic Center, and won the game against Minnesota, played at the Sports Center in Bloomington, by a score of 4-1. Murray was happy to end the two-game exhibition series with a win. Henry went back to Winnipeg and the Jets to play until February. He was confident he had made the National Team.

***

history again

During this time, the unfair practices over what was pro and amateur came to a head, with Canada withdrawing from the Tournament. The U.S. was asked to take Canada's place in the A group. The U.S. Olympic committee decided it would be best for the U.S. to stay in the B group category and play in Romania as planned.

***

February 6th Murray announced the dazzling eighteen players that would comprise the U.S. National Team for the 1970 International Competition.

Henry was ready to go when the final team gathered for some

training and two more pre-tournament games in the U.S. before they left. He wanted to get away from Debby's nagging and the perpetual fighting. He needed time to get his head unspun. He also wanted to play with the best, and this team Murray assembled had all the markings of just that.

Murray held a five-day training camp in Bloomington before they traveled to the northwestern corner of the state to play (and beat) the Warroad Lakers 5-4 in cold, flat, Thief River Falls -- a small hockey-loving town with a big heart -- on the stark prairies of Minnesota. Roger and Billy Christian, the former 1960 Gold Medal Olympians from Warroad, presented Henry with a watch from the Warroad Chamber of Commerce.

Back in Minneapolis, for a rematch with the University of Minnesota, the team did not fare so well. This time Glen Sonmor's Gophers beat them 5-4. The U of M roster included prime players: Mike Antonovich, Bruce McIntosh, Wally Olds, Don Ross and Craig Sarner. AHAUS officials were edgy over the loss, but, at the same time, felt assured Murray's Team hadn't had time to come together as a group yet.

Murray hoped his team would jell after the two exhibition games in Switzerland before the Tournament in Romania. The line-up included fifteen All-Americans and some of them made big marks in hockey history. One was the fabulous Herb Brooks, who very successfully coached the University of Minnesota and later went on to fame coaching the Golden 1980 Olympic team in Lake Placid, New York. Another was Craig Patrick, later general manager of the Pittsburgh Penguins.

Henry was the youngest on the team but, at eighteen, already commanded the respect of his teammates. He was humble -- all the press surprisingly hadn't managed to create a self-centered brat -- and was quiet and amazingly composed for his age. Thanks to the Jets, he was superlative as center: for scoring, assisting goals, and being everywhere at the right time. He was also tough on defense and used for strength on power plays. Henry never complained about anything and played either position with confidence.

Henry was a coach's dream and, much to Murray's delight, it was clear from the beginning that Henry was not only a highly skilled and great player, but he was also a team player.

Henry's years of working on his own to become technically perfect...followed by being recognized as the undisputed Star-of-the-North...led to the logical progression of hero to the state of Minnesota (bringing with it the hype that followed him at every turn). His months of being abused by the steely Jets' opposition, and coming out on top, had woven his fiber into a solid, exciting player. It all looked good from the outside, but Henry felt he was struggling. He suffered from a nervous stomach and was riddled with self-doubt. He kept with his philosophy of going with what he had, coupled with continually working on his skills.

Henry was also aware that he lacked manners and polish, and smart enough to know that he had to keep his eyes open and watch what others did in social situations. Henry was a fast learner in that area and was also an agreeable, interesting, well-behaved, likeable kid.

The eighteen-year-old Native American superstar who loved being close to home and family was about to become a globe-trotter. The kid who was married but so alone would become part of this team family. The boy who worked so hard to be the BEST and who wanted to play with the BEST he could was about to get his wish. It was the winter of 1970: Henry was about to take on the world.

first flight

When Henry stepped onto the plane that would carry the U.S. National Team to London and on to Switzerland, for two exhibition games against the Swiss National Team, and then on to the troubled city of Bucharest, Socialist Republic of Romania, for the International Games, he was the first of his family to fly across the ocean. It was technologies away from the early 1900's when his Ojibway mother and great-grandmother had concealed themselves from the Sioux in the reed-hidden canoe and when the warring stallions reared above his father at the Pow-Wow in the Indian village along the shore of Lake of the Woods.

armed neutrality

Murray's Team invaded neutral Switzerland, reputed a quiet land that conjured up images of *The Sound of Music*, mountains, cheese, good wine, chocolate and peaceful cows. His "team of stars" that bore the title of the U.S. National Team, did not have the bonding he knew they needed in order to play in sync and win in Romania. They had two more exhibition games to add that illusive all-important spice that picked up a team and set it on its heels. It was the hot pepper in nachos, the sugar in cake, the bite of a Pepsi, the hops in beer: the ingredient that gives it character and fastens it together.

Murray sensed the team was *trying* to unify. They were going through the motions of putting up that front: of being punctual and well informed, getting along with each other, playing sharp quick hockey and representing the United States as clean cut, intelligent athletes. It was an impressive group of young men who really were trying to bond.

Henry and Ozzie, now roommates, were inseparable and were dubbed Ozzie and Harriet by the team. Henry was non-plused about things the others considered front and center. Henry had no clue about what was expected or how he was to act. He didn't care about impressing anyone with who he was or where he came from. The others entered a rink as if they had sole ownership; Henry would wander into the locker room, usually last, casually, as if the exhibition games were pick-up games with the guys on the Warroad River. Inside himself, he was preparing for the game with steel like resolve; he just didn't show it on the outside.

Henry never followed suit by imitating or being someone else's idea of what a hockey player or a star or Henry Boucha should be. He was Henry Boucha and he was happy with who he was. He refused to be pretentious and had no intention of acting like anyone else. As the youngest player on the team, Henry became sort of a lovable younger brother to everybody.

The others were prepared in a way an observer could see. They were visually "ready" when they hit the ice; something they had absorbed from the Anglo-enculturation of their coaches and parents.

Once on ice Henry would skate around for warm-ups nonchalantly, as he always had done, even in the State Tournament. (His easy-going attitude drove his teammates nuts.) Then he would rev up silently, like a highly tuned Ferrari, and shift his gears up without anyone noticing to play his perfect hockey. He blended into the team as one of them, and did his brilliant stuff in a manner that the others had never seen before.

Murray understood Henry to a degree. He knew he was headed to the NHL and that the National Teams would round him out. Murray also knew there was something undefinable about Henry. He knew he marched to a drummer so different no one else could hear the beat. Murray didn't know about the Ojibway drums thumping in Henry's soul, but if he had he was the kind of person who would have understood.

Part of the weave of the U.S. teams was in knowing how to

have fun. The jokes the team members played on each other provided humor that was important to the team. There was the Ugly American Doll that a player had to carry for a full day when he "won" it. The doll was presented on silly trumped-up charges. One player would tell an exaggerated, embellished (outlandish) story on another player and the players would vote on the best story for who got the mask. The tales were hilarious and in good fun. The tradition was ridiculous, but it was a binding tool and everyone enjoyed it. Henry was given the doll for "knocking down an old woman who was trying to carry her food tray to her table."

In Geneva, the team rented a tour bus to go sightseeing the morning before their game. The other players showed up early and were enthusiastic about the trip. Henry and Ozzie had no intention of going; they slept in. Murray counted heads before the bus pulled out and realized "Ozzie and Harriet" weren't there. Murray did not believe in sleeping in. He was a firm believer in being up and with the program. He pounded on their door and yelled, "Get out of bed and out of that cave. We're goin' sight-seeing." Sleepily, the rumpled duo joined the others. They were glad they did; they were intrigued with the neat little farms, the tiny villages, the spire-topped mountains and the goats and cows with bells that roamed the picturesque, vertical hills.

That night, before a respectful crowd, Murray's U.S. Team played the Swiss National Team in a pre-tournament exhibition game. In a clean game they beat the Swiss 5-2. Murray was happy and the ever-hovering AHAUS officials were relieved. The Swiss were a team in the B group that would be faced in Romania. (The Japanese team, who had been training with the Czechs and who had been beating up on minor pro teams around Canada, were reputed to have the best team in the B group.)

The next day Murray's (happy) Team took a bus to the north of Switzerland to la Chaux-de-Fonds, to play the Swiss team in the second exhibition game. The manicured little farms impressed Henry again, as did the cobblestone streets in the villages. He never stopped asking the team doctor, Doc Nagobads, questions. "Hey, Doc," he would say and fire away. Doc liked the refreshing kid.

Finally the bus wound up the mountain road to la Chaux-de-Fonds and the players stepped out to a picturesque little ski village. It was so beautiful and the air was so perfect that it was almost lulling. They looked forward to another game playing the peaceful Swiss who had worked so hard for neutrality to protect themselves from their warring neighbors.

Murray's Team and Murray were in for a shock. Well before game time, the hyped-up wine-drinking fans found their seats and started screaming, blowing horns and winding themselves tight as a top so they could let go during the event. The soon-to-become-unruly mob was also a capacity crowd which, Murray figured out early in the game, was determined to run the game for the referees.

The Swiss went ahead 1-0 as their frenzied fans celebrated with more wine, screaming and horn blowing. The Europeans do not like the North American checking style of hockey, but Murray followed his game plan and played as the U.S. always did... checking in the corners and open ice. The Swiss resented it and howled in protest. Then, the Swiss *sweetheart* player, Michel Turler, was hit head-on by Konik and, as the crowd shrieked for revenge, Turler did it himself, lashing out at Konik with his stick. Both men received penalties.

The furious Swiss, reacting swiftly, torpedoed their plastic wine bottles...some empty, some partly empty and some full...to the ice. Ozzie, on the ice, was hit in the shoulder. Henry was on the bench. The boys on the bench scooted back as far as they could, to get their backs against the wood, flinging their arms over their heads in hopes of some protection, as bottles bounced off their knees.

Once the Swiss started there was no stopping them; the yelling and jeering and bottle-showers continued pelting the U.S. players as they tried to dodge them. The boys couldn't understand what the crowd was yelling at them...but they could guess.

The score was 3-3 at the end of the second period, but as the boys gathered in the locker room between periods, Murray saw an unforeseen miracle. He saw it in their eyes. He saw it in their genuine togetherness as they exchanged bottle stories. He saw, that like little globes of mercury on a plate, rolling toward center to make one shimmery sphere, the 1970 National players had bonded.

Henry played the third period trying not to annoy any Swiss player and keeping out of their way lest he upset the crowd into sending something more lethal than a plastic wine bottle his way. It was unnerving and totally frightening playing to such a malicious crowd and far worse than anything he had ever encountered with the Jets.

The Swiss scored on a power play and Hibbing's Gary Gambucci answered the goal with one for the U.S. The score remained tied 4-4. With thirty seconds left in regulation play,

Gambucci got the puck and was on his way with a breakaway when a Swiss player tripped him. The Swiss was penalized and the bottles flew again. The German referee did not have the guts to call for a penalty shot. Murray thought he had done well to even call the penalty. The game was delayed for clean-up.

With the U.S. gaining the power play, the chance for scoring was better. Henry, who never got rattled, and who hated to lose, got control of the puck in the last five seconds and fired it, definite and calculatingly, across ice to George Konik, who was clear and in good scoring position. George grabbed the puck on the end of his stick, aimed past the goalie and fired it in. The angry Swiss fans gave all they had left to punish the Americans, but it didn't matter. Murray's Team had proved it could play, and play well enough to win in the pressure-cooker, against the bottle-armed and very unneutral Swiss fans.

With a smile and a song in his heart, Murray knew his team was ready for Bucharest in Romania. His team was ready to take on the Japanese, the Yugoslavians, the Germans and every other team in the B group.

endangered species

Traveling behind the iron curtain in the early '70's was traveling back in time to a weird, oppressed place, dressed in gray, where a person from a free country couldn't find his center of balance. There was no familiar point of reference to our taken-for-granted free society. Strange things happened to people. Hundreds of thousands had been killed by Stalin in the '50's. Spies were prevalent; no one could trust anyone else. It was a Communist dictatorship in the worse sense of the word, and it was scary.

Doc Nagobads knew this from experience. He had escaped from Latvia in the '50's and fled to Germany to earn his medical degree. He took those medical school tests in German. Then he pushed on to the U.S., where he had to retake grueling exams in English. Doc tried to explain to the team the severity of the situation in Bucharest -- and behind the iron curtain -- and the bitter hostility nations were having toward one another, but his warnings were always lost on the boys.

On the bus traveling from la Chaux-de-Fonds to Zurich, the sunny day after the bottle pelting, the mood was ecstatic. The happy-go-lucky hockey players weren't tuned in to Doc's gloom. They were busy trumping up charges with their little "devil" doll, thinking up harmless pranks, enjoying the "high" that went with the bonding, and escaping injury at the hands of the Swiss mob.

The driver of the tour bus received a call that halted the festivities. He was informed that an Israeli plane had been bombed and there was reason to feel the American National Team was also on the endangered species list. The bus was to proceed to Zurich, where it was being arranged for the players to get through customs incognito and board their plane on the tarmac before the terrorists could figure out where they were. For this plan to be successful, everything had to be done as hastily as possible. The stunned players stopped joking and girded themselves for the task ahead.

In Zurich the bus driver dropped the apprehensive players off at the airport with warnings to be very quiet and very careful. They were herded through customs, snuck onto the tarmac and up the rickety stairs to an antiquated Romanian plane. Herb Brooks did not want to get on and Murray had to use his powers of persuasion again. The last man was barely into the plane when the door slammed behind him. The pilot wasted no time. The careening plane roared down the runway as they were taking their seats, and lifted off as they were buckling in. In his move to avoid possible gunfire, he headed the plane nearly straight up into the safety of the blue above. The craft convulsed in protest, the team rattled inside it like a chicken leg being shook in a *Shake and Bake* bag and Doc thought out loud, "I hope this plane lasts." To a man the players, including Henry, were terrified. The rest of the flight was unsettling but the plane landed safely, and unannounced, behind the clamped-shut iron curtain in Bucharest, the capital of Romania.

Bucharest

Having made it through this harrowing experience, the group felt giddy. As it happened, Henry was riding between Doc and Murray on the bus from the tarmac where the plane had parked to the Bucharest airport and customs. Doc decided to start off the fun. He leaned across Henry and said to Murray, as he felt his breast pocket, "I've got my papers, you got yours?" Murray, always ready for a good joke, answered in his best deadpan, "Of course, they won't let us through without them. We'd be thrown in jail and never see home again." The others picked up on this and were all confidently feeling their pockets. Henry didn't have his papers. He had given his to Murray. All the players had given their passports and visas to Murray but were going along with the joke on Henry. Henry started sweating: he was worried. He was sure he had given his papers to Murray, but he didn't say anything. Someone broke out laughing and Henry realized the joke was pointed at him. Always the good sport, Henry laughed too. Everyone was feeling the needed comic relief.

Once in the airport the boys let loose with their own jokes. When they lined up for customs, stoic Russian military circled the room with practiced glares and big guns. It was an odd experience as the Russians were the same age as the young men on Murray's Team. The boys didn't take the cue. One said to the unflappable soldiers, "Doc has $1,000,000 with him, you shouldn't let him through." Doc realized the gravity of this and tried to shush the boys, who were getting into this prank. Another piped up, "Don't think we'll be seein' Doc again. They'll take him to Latvia." Doc was really sweating in earnest and desperately trying to shut them up, but, like the Swiss and their bottles, the boys were on a roll. Doc got through, no thanks to the pranksters: the Russians had no idea what they were saying.

The mood in Romania was dismal: the feeling hopeless. They were a beaten people going through the motions of living; who looked out from hollowed eye sockets set in dingy, colorless faces.

The bus pulled up to an "Old Glory" hotel where the team was staying. It was imposing on the outside, but inside the lobby there were big spots on the walls and the beautiful old tapestry wallpaper was peeling off. "What's the smell?" Henry said. "Mildew," Doc sadly answered the undirected question. He knew how grand this hotel had once been, but now either no one cared or they didn't have the energy or money to fix it.

Doc warned the boys to be very cautious. He warned them about spies. He warned them to be careful what they said and particularly not to do anything illegal. The boys didn't believe him, but Doc knew first-hand how Communists were.

Doc wanted to take the boys to a Gypsy restaurant. He asked an old man he saw on the street where a good one was. The old man started crying when Doc asked him. The man sputtered out that unfortunately they no longer existed. He said no one wanted to go out anymore because one never knew whom he was sitting next to. Informers were everywhere. It wasn't safe.

Hi-jinx expert, Herb Books, loved a good joke. One day Ozzie and Henry were in their room. The phone rang. Henry answered it. On the other end he heard a man with a Swedish accent who said he wanted to see the hockey equipment of the Americans and could they please come down with some. Ozzie and Henry, happy to oblige, took a few items down and sat in the lobby. They waited and they waited. Herb Brooks and Carl Wetzel walked through and asked what they were doing. They told them they were waiting for the Swedes. The other players, who were hiding behind columns and plants in the lobby, kept emerging and passing by them - one by one. After a very long wait with no Swedes, Henry and Ozzie finally realized they'd been had.

The first game was an 11-1 U.S. team blow-out against the highly ranked Japanese team. Time to celebrate! One down, six to go!

Konik

The legal money exchange from U.S. currency to Romanian was a rip-off in Bucharest. George Konik, the oldest team member, was a bit of a fable in his own right. He was an All-American. He had won MVP of the tough Saskatchewan Hockey League. He had played with the Flin Flon Bombers, winners of the prestigious Memorial Cup. He could speak Ukranian and nosed around until he found a Romanian who would exchange U.S. currency at a rate twice the bank's. To Konik this only made good sense, but this was clearly black market activity and very dangerous. Konik had done it twice for himself and other players.

At supper one night, several teammates asked him to do it again. Konik said a good-natured, "Sure," and set up the appointment. He went alone to the apartment building at the designated time. It was very dark as he climbed the spiral staircase to meet his contact on an upper level. Konik and the Romanian did the exchange and went down the stairs and back outside -- where they were greeted by three men wearing black coats. Konik thought, "Oh shit," but there was nothing he could do. The men, who turned out to be Romanian policeman, confiscated the money and took Konik and the Romanian to police headquarters in a police jeep. En route, the frightened Romanian money-changer told Konik he would have to go before a Tribunal; his future looked bleak. Konik never heard of him or from him again.

Konik was taken to a room with a long table for interrogation where he kept pointing at his USA hockey crest. Konik was a colorful player and very popular with the fans. Within half an hour Konik was a free man. The Romanians were not about to start an international crisis over this issue.

An angry Murray was waiting for Konik when he got back. As Konik wasn't where he was supposed to be, when he was supposed to be, Murray had extracted his whereabouts from his teammates. Murray was not relishing a nasty encounter with the Romanian authorities or having to explain to the AHAUS officials why one of their players was in a Romanian jail. Murray warned Konik that he would be sent home if he misbehaved again.

the Romanian games

The Romanian games were attended by men only, and a great many of them were from the military. It was odd for the team-members to look up at the sea of male faces. The last game was attended by one lone woman -- the commander's wife.

Murray's Team swept the B tournament by beating Japan, Bulgaria, Switzerland, Yugoslavia, Romania, West Germany and Norway. Henry had learned with the seasoned players. They talked to him on the ice and told him what to do. They taught him patience with the puck and when to go and when not to. It was a great group of guys, on and off the ice.

At the end of the game, a Romanian folk band came out on the ice to entertain with an American tune they had prepared for the event. The players expected the National Anthem or a favorite American show tune but instead, of all the American songs they could have selected, they chose *Whatever Lola Wants, Lola Gets*. The players thought this was a hoot. Then Romanian women appeared and poured champagne over the players' heads. It ended up being a hilarious ending to the '70 Nationals' trip.

The U.S. National Team was back in the A bracket. They also won the Fair Play Cup for the team with the least number of penalties...a rarity in U.S. hockey history.

Murray had done a splendid job and so had his team. On a personal level, Henry came back a much-improved player. He had played with the best amateurs in the U.S. and done well under the very intelligent and caring coaching of Murray, who considered himself a student of Tarasov. Henry had played the emotional hockey that he loved. He had kept his eyes open to learn what he could socially, educationally and ice-wise. He had skated with older, smarter players, and Henry felt the flow and sync of working as a team that he had never known before. Now he was ready to rejoin the Winnipeg Jets for the last three weeks of Western Canada Hockey League play.

Rome

The Romanian trip took a toll on everyone's body. Most of the players lost 10-15 pounds over the two-week period of sub-standard food and water. The water was so bad no one was drinking it: Coca-Cola was flown in from London for the team.

Murray had told them if they were undefeated in National play he would take them to Rome. For three days the team ate and basked in Rome. To Henry it was spectacular.

Flin Flon

Henry went back to the Jets for the last games of the season. It was good to be back with his peers, and it was good for the team to have his hard shot and quick stick. He was moving the puck better after his National Team experience, and the help of the older guys. In the playoffs against Estevan, Saskatchewan, the Jets beat them four straight.

Then they faced the Flin Flon Bombers, a team in a remote town almost five hundred miles north of Winnipeg. The people of Flin Flon prided themselves in surviving the raw elements of the North. The Bombers hated the Winnipeg (city) team and were always out to prove their superiority. Reggie Leach and Blaine Stout (later to be fifty-goal scorers in the NHL) were on the team along with Genen Carr from B.C. It was a best-of-nine series. In Flin Flon the fans would be drinking: mildly at first, wildly later. They would hang over the boards, grabbing and holding any Jet they could get their hands on. There was brawl after brawl in the games. The Jets were victorious the four games in Winnipeg. The Bombers won the four games in turbulent Flin Flon. Now it was down to the last game, played in Flin Flon. It was so wild in the arena the fans were scary. The game went into overtime. Henry hit the pipe...and then a Flin Flon player scored. The game was over just like that. The season was over...and although he didn't know it then, the Jets were over for Henry.

24

Uncle Sam

Henry went home to little Warroad, on the edge of Lake of the Woods, for the summer. In the months he was away, he had made a metamorphosis from a not fully drawn kid to a definable young man. He planned to return to the Jets in the fall, play with the '71 Nationals and finish with the Jets again. It had been a perfect year hockey-wise and he planned to repeat it. He got a job with Marvin Windows and took up golf to keep away from Debby. He felt like a contented tomcat lying in the sun licking his fur.

Life was good...and summer *was* progressing nicely until the letter from Uncle Sam arrived, informing him his lottery draft number was #36 and up to two hundred dates would be pulled. The Vietnam War was still raging. Boys, who had never had any violence in their lives, were being plucked like rocks and dropped into the dark well, many never to return and more to return minus limbs and sound minds. Every draft-age eligible and his loved ones lived in terrible fear of this, and now Henry was confronted with it. He was devastated. He didn't want to be dropped into the well. The casualties in Vietnam were horrendous and no thinking person could see for what purpose.

***

selective service

The Selective Service pulled birth dates from a lottery draft. In 1970, two hundred birth dates were being pulled to fill the nearly 400,000 troops "needed" that year to fulfill the U.S. military commitment in Vietnam.

***

Henry called Murray. Murray called the Pentagon, then called Henry back and told him the best way to go would be to enlist now and go into the Army in August. That way he could get boot camp out of the way and be eligible to play on the National Team, on loan from the Army, after boot camp. This was a wrenching way to realize he would never join his buddies on the Jets again.

On August 20th Henry reported to Ft. Knox, Kentucky. While in the reception center for two weeks, waiting for the next rotation of boot camp to start, someone broke into his locker and stole his belongings.

Next, Henry did a curious thing. He was always the go-along-to-get-along-guy, who just never made waves; but, of the two hundred and fifty recruits in his outfit, Henry was the only one who refused to get his head shaved. He got his hair cut short, but not shaved. Because of this stubbornness he was on Kitchen Patrol every day hauling garbage, etc. He got in a cycle...the Drill Sergeant would send him down to get his hair cut...Henry would go to the PX and look around, come back without it cut and be put back on KP duty or picking up cigarette butts. It got to be a regular thing, with his counterparts encouraging him, egging him on and telling him not to get it shaved.

Henry endorsed all his checks over to Debby and sent them back to her in Warroad. He didn't even have change to buy an ice cream cone.

A rumor circulated in his barracks that Henry was going to be playing for the U.S. National Hockey Team. When asked about it he said, "Yes," and that he had been on last year's National Team. "Yeah, right," they answered. To make matters worse, the First Sergeant, a grizzly thirty-year man, hated athletes and thought that playing hockey *for the Army* was "bullshit." In the physical drills Henry always came out way ahead of everyone else. This irritated the Sergeant, who gave him more KP duty than ever. This just made Henry more determined. He tried to stay quiet and out of the limelight.

In the world of his mind, he vacillated between dreaming of the upcoming National Team, and playing with the best again, and feeling chills of depression coupled with the fear that Murray wouldn't call. His life was clear before him: he would either fall into a vast abyss or go to the glory of the International Competition. It was the longest ten weeks of his life.

Finally, the orders came from the Pentagon to join the National Team for tryouts in Minnesota. Henry was out of there, and back to Minneapolis, away from the First Sergeant and safe in the home of his brother David.

When Henry hit the ice with the National Team, he hadn't played hockey since the last hairy Flin Flon game with the Jets. He was clearly out of skating shape. Worse yet, he was staying many miles from the arena and had no car. As he had no money for bus fare (Debby was still getting his Army checks) he had to hitchhike. When he would get to the rink late Murray wouldn't let him skate. This threw Henry into a panic, but he never told Murray he was broke. He lived in quiet dread that he would not be selected for the National Team.

25

Step one was behind Murray: a super showing in the '70 Nationals, which qualified them for the A group in Switzerland in '71. Step two, placing high on the qualifiers in group A in 'Switzerland in '71 to assure an easy qualifying round in the Japan Olympics in '72, was smack in front of them. Murray knew what was ahead of them and selected his team carefully. He also put together the toughest schedule he could, playing top college and semi-pro oppositions. The higher a team would finish in the Swiss Worlds in '71, the easier it would be to win the qualifying -- 1st round -- of the Olympic games. Thus, the U.S. wanted to place high so they could play an easy team in the qualifying round in Sapporo in '72. What Murray didn't know was that this team would be plagued with injuries.

McGlynn

The invitations went out for tryouts for the National Team. Henry got his, via his Army Orders, but Dick McGlynn, from Boston, who attended Colgate College, was not on the list. Dick decided to pack up his hockey equipment and go to the rink where tryouts were being held in Boston. He saw a man standing by the ice and asked him who he was. "Murray Williamson, the coach of this team," Murray answered, eyeing McGlynn's bag. "Who are you?" "I'm Dick McGlynn and I'm going to be one of your players," Dick retorted. Murray was so taken aback he told him to go to the locker room and get dressed.

At the end of tryouts, Murray told McGlynn he would be the eighth defenseman on the team and that while he probably wouldn't see any ice time, he could practice with the team. McGlynn said, "Fine, all I want is a chance."

Back in Minnesota, Murray told McGlynn he would get an apartment for him: McGlynn had to pay half of the rent and the team would pay the other half, for the apartment to be used as a "wait station" for boys who would be trying out for the team. McGlynn had many Olympic-hopefuls through the revolving door, but he was lonesome. The other players were either married or had roommates. Twenty years later, when he gave a short speech at the Olympic reunion, McGlynn thought enough of Henry to talk about how kind Henry was to the new kid on the block, and how much Henry's friendship meant to him.

gearing up

So, as Murray gathered his players, he felt as he had last year...that they needed some games to quicken the jelling process. He set up contests against any stiff competition (junior teams and colleges) he could, and was pleased when Omaha (then the New York Rangers' farm club) agreed to play them. Tough guys Moose Dupont, Jack Egers, Steve Durbano, and Rick Newell "showed up" when the prima donna U.S. Team came; their goal was to carve them up. During the game, Henry was sucker-punched and had to be stitched up. A player on the Omaha team yelled, "If he's that dumb to stand and get punched down, don't give him Novocaine!" Murray had had it. He decided to do some intimidating of his own and sent out *his* tough guy, Tim Sheehy, to rough Newell up. Murray was ejected for screaming (in his words, protesting) that it was the refs who were being intimidated. He was not present when Kevin Ahern, from Boston College, scored the winning goal for the U.S. team.

Thanksgiving they played Cornell University. The boys were homesick, being away from their families on the holiday. The team was escorted to rotten accommodations: a dark and deserted dorm, four boys to a room with plank-style bunk beds. Murray was upset; he insisted the boys be put up in a hotel. Murray had requested practice ice time but was told there was no ice time slated for the team. (Later he found out that the practice ice allotted for his team had stood empty.) The Cornell coach, Dick Bertram, afraid he would lose the game, refused to play by International Rules (a condition which was agreed upon prior to the game). The U.S. team needed to practice using those rules.

Then, Cornell was to pay $2,500 to the U.S. team. An Olympic vice president, Bob Kane, was also the athletic director at Cornell. Instead of the agreed upon $2,500, Cornell paid $500! (Eventually the U.S. Olympic team received $1,500 more to "avoid further allegations that he (Kane) was 'using the Olympic team to fatten the coffers of Cornell'." Quote from "The Great American Hockey Dilemma." Murray Williamson, 1978.) The Nationals beat the previously undefeated Cornell, even with Cornell's own rules!

The team did well in pre-season: Murray felt happy, and secure in his choices, as they headed over the Atlantic for the '71 games.

Carl Wetzel, who later played for the North Stars, was signed on as #1 goalie. Lefty Curran, from the University of North Dakota, was back-up goalie. The team liked and trusted him. In the last pre-season game against the University of Minnesota Gophers, Curran injured his knee. Back then, knee injuries couldn't be diagnosed like they are today. The doctor and trainer thought it would be O.K. and put him on crutches to rest it. No one thought much of it. Give it some time off and it will be fine, was the general consensus.

Prague

The plane landed in the spectacular, then behind-the-iron-curtain city of Prague, Czechoslovakia, for the exhibition game with the Czechs. Henry always felt that being behind the iron curtain was scary. This city, built on the romantic Vltava River with an imposing castle looking down on it, may well be the most beautiful city in Europe, but then it was dark and oppressive with the Communist Regime in control. In 1918 the freedom-loving Czechs established a Western-style government in Prague. Hitler stopped all that by marching in on them and gaining control in 1939, and then the Soviets oppressed the Czechs after WWII. In 1968 they tried again for freedom, and failed.

The team had been traveling for sixteen hours and the players were exhausted. To make it worse, with the time change, Prague was seven hours later than Minnesota time. A much-needed night's sleep to recoup was before them. The game was tomorrow night...so Murray thought. Murray called his hockey contact to inform him the team had arrived only to find out the grim news the game was *that* night. A sick-at-heart Murray herded his weary team to the old Prague hotel that reminded them of the hotel in Bucharest a year before. He knew the Czechs were going to be tough to meet rested and now his team had to face them without proper sleep. He gathered the team together for a quick team meeting and laid out the rules, including not going to the bar on the top floor of the hotel. That was off-limits: verboten/forbidden. He told them all to go to their rooms and get what little rest they could before they had to board the bus to the Czech rink.

As soon as the team meeting was over and Murray and the others headed for some bed rest, Konik and Henry headed straight for the elevator to the top floor bar to see what was shakin'. It was odd because the elevator opened up right into the bar. Through sign language they made friends with the bartender, who knew they weren't supposed to be there. The beer was the worst they'd ever tasted but it was fun to be where

Murray didn't want them to be.

Soldiers, dressed in old military outfits, meandered around the hotel. A movie called *Slaughterhouse 5* was being filmed there by an American film company.

***

The big old Czech arena was filled to capacity with 15,000 fans. (The same number as the Edina-Warroad game of games two years earlier.) The Czechs were ranked #2 in the world and, after spending a week in their mountain retreat training camp, were pumped to take on the Americans. They were flying all over the ice in warm-ups. It wasn't a good feeling for the blurry-eyed U. S. boys who stood and watched them warming up. Curran's knee had to be shot up with Novocaine.

The Czech team scored four unanswered goals in eight minutes. Murray, dazed, got his wits about him and decided the only tactic left was intimidation and heavy hitting to slow the Czechs down. The Europeans, not liking Murray's plan, started whistling whenever the U.S. checked one of their players. Gary Gambucci hit a Czech, resulting in knocking the Czech's teeth out. The fans went into a rage against the U.S. team, blowing a deafening shrill whistle that made the U.S. players' ears buzz and gave them crushing headaches. Murray's approach worked; the Czechs only reaped two more goals in the game. The good news was that the Americans knew they could hold the Czechs by intimidation tactics. The bad news was that Curran was having problems with his knee.

After the game, when they got back to the hotel, Konik and Henry headed to the forbidden bar to console themselves. As they were happily sipping the awful beer, they saw the bartender waving frantically. They looked in time to see Murray and Buddy, the equipment manager, getting off the elevator and walking toward the bar. Konik and Henry hit the floor under the table and crawled on their bellies under tables until they got close to the bar. They lay there listening to Murray talking to Buddy about lines. Murray and Buddy took their drinks to a table, backs turned toward the elevator and bar. The bartender gave them an all-clear signal and they crawled out of the bar and onto the elevator when it opened. With a sigh of relief, they descended to safety.

Henry hooked up with Tom Mellor in the lobby. They were just nosing around the hotel following some '50 Elvis music. They trailed it to a ballroom filled with dancing Czech teenagers. It was weird because the teens were dressed in '50's clothes. This wasn't part of a movie, just the behind-the-times Eastern European clothes. The boys decided to go in and see what was going on. The duo sat down and had a great time making fun of the clothes and the music. A Czech girl at the next table listened to them for awhile – before she asked them a question in English. The sheepish, very embarrassed boys exited the scene.

Bern

The next day the team traveled to Switzerland for the World Championship. There were to be ten games: five played in Bern, the other five in Geneva. Henry was relieved to be out from under the iron curtain, and he was happy to go to clean and lovely Bern, Switzerland.

The hotel was nestled high on the mountainside outside the beautiful town. The team had to take a tram to get up there, so it was loaded with mystique and loveliness. The clear Swiss air and tidy, colorful countryside were most welcome after shaded-gray, oppressive Prague. The Russian team stayed at the same hotel. While they were eating breakfast, the U.S. players watched the Soviets play soccer in the parking lot. Later, from the windows of their rooms, they watched them run the up and down the mountains behind the hotel. The Russian coach, Tarasov, made sure his team was always on the go and had little down time.

The first game in the World Tournament was against the Czechs. Murray was ready for them this time. He planned a heavy hitting, physical game. The Czechs retreated every time they got near the blue line, regrouping for their passing plays. The U.S. was ready with intimidation. Valclav Nedomansky, the Czechs' prime celebrity player, took a slap shot. Henry deflected it by blocking it. The puck bounced off Henry and landed behind Nedomansky. Henry took off like greased lightning, snapped up the puck and went tearing off down ice with it, setting it neatly behind the goalie. The U.S. scored 4 more goals to the Czechs' 1. Murray's Team was on the road with a nice victory in their pocket. Curran had to play with his knee numbed again.

After the game, Tarasov came to congratulate them. He grabbed Murray with both hands on his jaw and gave Murray a big kiss. This was very amusing to the team.

Sweden was the next hurdle. Murray's Team was watching the Russians play another team before their game against the

Swedes. The score of the Russian game was 0-0 at the end of the 1st period, which was not acceptable to Tarasov. As the other team retreated to the dressing room congratulating itself that the Russians had not scored against them, Tarasov marched his team to an adjoining empty rink and made them do rigorous starts and stops for the entire period break. The Russians went on to beat their opposition.

The U.S. was tied with the Swedish team 2-2. Wetzel was injured. The hot-dog Mike Curran was in the nets. Henry got the puck and a breakaway halfway through the 3rd period. His score was classic Henry...and would have made his fans at home *oooooooooohhhhhhhh.* The referee, who was trapped down at the other end, ruled a no-goal (offside) because one of the U.S. players was sitting on the boards with his foot hanging over, waiting for a line change. Three minutes later the Swedes scored to go ahead and at the end of game the Swedes got an empty netter. Curran's knee was shot up again and he was unhappy because 1) he was worried about more injury to his knee and 2) he felt he wasn't bringing his play to the ice because of the injury. It was sad for Murray to lose the game but he also had the loss of Konik, who got injured and consequently was out for the next four games, and Craig Patrick, who hurt his back. That wasn't the end of it. Lefty Curran said flatly he wouldn't play any more games. This news, on top of the pain of an unjust defeat, was terrible for Murray, who had his plan worked out so well only to see it bombed by circumstances beyond his control.

There was little hope of beating Russia; it was a matter of hanging in there. Murray's tactics for this game were to slow the game down with as many whistles and delays as possible. It didn't work. The Russians creamed them 10-2 and morale fell. The team went on to lose to the Finns and Germans. Their record for the first half of the tournament was 1 win and 4 losses.

Geneva

Murray's troupe was on their way to Geneva for the second half of the tournament and a party hosted for them by Hank Ketcham, cartoonist of *Dennis the Menace,* and golden actor of the times, William Holden. The party was held at the posh Geneva Golf Club. This was great for the boys' morale and, the next day, they held the Russian team to only a two-goal win: Russians 7, Americans 5. The game was exciting and the boys were feeling happy and confident again.

With both Carl Wetzel and Mike Curan injured, the third goalie, Dick Tomasoni, manned the nets for the rest of the tournament.

The U.S. lost to the Finns, Swedes and Czechs. They beat Germany but not by enough goals to keep them out of last place. They were on the bottom of the A pile going into the 1972 Olympics, which would be held in Sapporo, Japan, the following winter.

U.S. 1971 National Team

*Murray Williamson's 1971 U.S. National Team included Henry, Huffer Christianson, Kevin Ahern, Dick Toomey, Len Lilyholm, Carl Wetzel, Dick Tomasoni, Don Ross, Gary Gambucci, George Konik, Lefty Curran, Dick McGlynn, Tom Mellor, Jim McElmury, Tim Sheehy, Bruce Riutta, Craig Falkman, Craig Patrick, Paul Shilling, Bob Lindberg, Don Neiderkorn, and Pete Fishuk.

26

Army

Henry was allowed to go back to Warroad for a brief visit before he had to return to Army life. Then he hitched a ride to the Twin Cities on a Marvin Windows truck so he could catch the plane in Minneapolis that would take him to Military Police School at Ft. Gordon, Georgia.

While in M.P. school, where he was learning how to shoot and drive a jeep, John Gilbert from the *Minneapolis Star* called him that he had been selected by the Detroit Red Wings 16th overall (2nd round) in the NHL draft.

As graduation from M.P. school was nearing, the talk was that all two hundred and fifty in Henry's group were headed to Vietnam. Henry called Murray again. Murray said, "Don't worry about it." Henry went home briefly when M.P. schooling was over. It was miserable with Debby again. She had taken to scratching his arms, so he had to wear long-sleeve shirts to hide the embarrassing scratches. He was glad to go to his next placement: Germany.

Germany was a nice place to be. Henry's job was to check the gates of the Missile Army Depot. He drove around in a jeep and liked the job and the people he was stationed with. He was nine days on and three days off, which suited his style.

When Henry got called into the Captain's office, in the fall of '71, the Captain was looking at orders. Henry sensed they were his and his heart skipped a beat to be going back on the ice again. "Are these right?" the Captain asked Henry. Henry assured him they were and that he was going to be on the '72 Olympic Hockey Team in Sapporo, Japan. The Captain had never met an Olympic athlete before and thought it was *really* cool. Soon after, an article came out about Henry in the Army's newspaper, *Stars and Stripes*.

Jonathan Morrisseau, Henry's great-grandfather. Jonathan was a Canadian Treaty-Indian. He was a voyageur for the Hudson Bay Company. Jonathan was Henry's grandmother, Rebecca's, father. *circa 1940*

Joseph Boucha, Henry's grandfather, owned Painted Rock Narrows fish camp and the floating barge that carried goods to the settlements on the shore of Lake of the Woods. Shown here are Joseph and Rebecca. The two older girls are their daughters, Irene, the younger, and Elvina. The two little girls are cousins. *circa 1940*

Indian ladies at Buffalo Point. Henry's mother, Alice, is fourth from the right. Henry's great-grandmother, Laughing Mary, is on the far left. *circa 1927*

Henry's father, George, second from left and Alice, next to George. Little Georgie is standing in front of Alice. *circa 1943*

One-year-old Henry in his wagon. 1952

Year-and-a-half-old Henry with his siblings and dog, Purp. Brother, Jim, is holding on to Henry. Shirley, David and Georgie stand behind them. 1952

Happy times. Family fishing expedition on Georgie's fifteenth birthday. Shirley, Georgie, David and Darlene on the boat and Henry and George are below steering the craft. 1954

Three-year-old Henry and his father George on the fishing boat. 1954

Cousin, Irene Boucha Bobczynski, and Henry's sister, Phyllis. 1956

Brothers Jimmy, Eddie and Henry at home in Warroad.

Alice, Henry and Eddie relaxing.

Ten-year-old Henry ready for baseball.

Henry *oooooooohhhhhhhhing* the Minnesota State High School Tournament fans in the game against Roseau. 1969

The Warroad Warriors, 1969. Back row: coach Roberts, M. Marvin, R. Ellerbusch, S. Helmstetter, M. Hanson, captain H. Boucha, F. Krahn, J. Hodgson, L. Kvarnlov, T. Stukel, assistant coach Dale Telle, G. Pieper. Front row: E. Huerd, J. Taylor, R. Estling, J. Hallett, R. Marshall, L. Marshall, A. Hangsleben, R. Storey.

Henry Boucha.
1969

Edina's Jim Knutson's hit. Championship game of the Minnesota State High School Tournament. 1969

Winnipeg Junior A Jets.

The 1970 U.S. National Team in an airport. Left to right: Huffer Christianson, coach Murray Williamson, Lenny Lillyholm, Gary Gambucci, Pete Markle, Ozzie O'Neill, Gary Johnson, trainer Doc Rose, general manager Hal Trumble, George Konik, Jim McElmury, Bruce Riutta, Henry, Carl Wetzel, Larry Stordahl, Charlie Brown, Craig Patrick, Bob Fleming (chairman of AHAUS), Don Ross, Bob Lindberg, Herb Brooks, public relations G. Anderson, Brian Grand, and team doctor, Doc Nagobads.

Romanian Officers watching the U.S. Team. 1970

1972 Olympic games, Sapporo, Japan. The U.S. Team is playing the Russians. Mike Curran is in the nets. Henry #10. Frank Sanders #9 and Jim McElmury #2.

"Hot-dog" Mike Curran making the save. Sapporo, Japan. 1972

The 1972 Silver Olympians. First row: Pete Sears, Keith Christianson, coach Murray Williamson, manager Hal Trumble, Tim Sheehy, Mike Curran. Second row: equipment manager Buddy Kessel, Bruce McIntosh, Jim McElmury, Larry Bader, Frank Sanders, Ron Naslund, Wally Olds, Charlie Brown, Tim Regan, Dr. Nagobads. Back row: Mark Howe, Craig Sarner, Tom Mellor, Henry, Dick McGlynn, Kevin Ahearn, Robbie Ftorek, Stu Irving.

Baby Tara

"Chief" Red Wing.

1st NHL goal. March 22, 1972. Henry #12 white.

Red Wing Henry in action against the New York Rangers.

1973-'74 Detroit Red Wings. First row: Jim Norris, Doug Grant, Nick Libbet, general manager Ned Harkness, Bruce Norris, Alex Delvecchio, Nick Redmond, Terry Richardson, Jim Skinner. Second row: team attorney John Ziegler, Lefty Smith, Guy Charron, Doug Roberts, Tommie Bergman, Ted Harris, Ron Stackhouse, Billy Collins, Henry, Ace Bailey. Third row: trainer Tommy (last name unknown), Tom Mellor, Brent Hughes, Larry Johnson, Red Barrenson, Tord Lundstrom, Marcel Dionne, trainer Dan Olesevich.

Red Wings vs. Chicago Blackhawks. Henry scores on Tony Esposito.

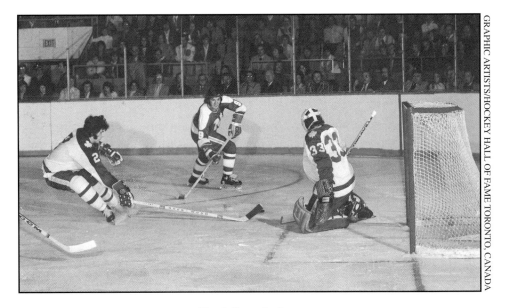

1974-'75 Minnesota North Stars. Bottom row: Cesare Maniago, Barry Gibbs, Dennis Hextall, assistant general manager Charlie Burns, president Walter Bush, coach Jack Gordon, Bill Goldsworthy, J.P. Parise, Peter LoPresti. Second row: trainer Dennis Kovach, Richard Nantais, Dennis O'Brien, Henry, Tom Reid, Doug Hicks, Fred Stanfield, trainer Dick Rose. Third row: Jude Drouin, Lou Nanne, Blake Dunlop, Chris Ahrens, John Flesch, Don Martineau, Fred Barrett, Murray Oliver.

North Stars Action.

Henry at work: North Stars.

The North Stars fending off the Boston Bruins. Part of Henry can be seen under the referee.

Randi and Henry. News conference.

27

'72 Olympics: Japan

training camp

Henry flew from Ramstein Air Base in Germany to Charleston, South Carolina, en route to the Olympic tryout camp in Bemidji, Minnesota. He and two other Army guys he didn't know stayed overnight in Charleston. In the morning, Henry got up to catch his flight back to Minneapolis and the last team of Murray's (and Henry's) U.S.A. trilogy. The other two soldiers were gone...and so was Henry's ticket and any money he had in his wallet. Henry was nearly flat broke with $2 in his pocket. He called team manager, Hal Trumble, collect. Hal replaced Henry's ticket.

Murray secured a cabin for Henry and his pregnant wife, Debby, to live in for the two weeks of tryouts. It should have been an idyllic situation, but the arguing started immediately, turning into ugly fights. Henry was not able to get the rest he needed. Henry, not about to put up with having his tryout compromised, moved to other quarters.

It was Henry's aim to keep up his childhood, high school, Jets and National Team level by his habit of always working hard but, unfortunately, he hadn't been on skates for months. He skated practice relentlessly, pushing his body as far as it would go. Then at night he would soak his legs in the bathtub to get rid of the stiffness. Henry did not let his energy flag. He was a self-starter and knew no other way than to always be the maximum he could be. He worked to the same level in warm-ups, in tryouts and later in the games. These tough Indian Warrior attributes were why Henry was a world-class athlete.

Murray held three tryout camps: Detroit, Boston and Bemidji. Twenty players made it onto his first roster, but during the fall players came and went as Murray changed his mind. This had to be the most perfect team he could amass.

He was always concerned about lines: in creating the perfect balance with the elements he had. In watching the Russian players he figured they were stronger than the U.S. hockey athletes, but not necessarily bigger. He had visited Tarasov in Russia over the summer to find out how the Soviet camp was run, and came back armed with a conditioning program.

After the tryouts in Bemidji, the team went to Minneapolis for a two-week training camp at the DeCathlon Club. They skated at the Met Center twice a day to keep up their skating skills...at high speed, game tempo. Murray wanted them stuffing themselves with high-quality, high-calorie foods. He said that they needed to eat better than the "beer and pizza leagues." Meal times were the fun part of the day. It was then that important bonding took place. The players ate at the training tables and played jokes on each other. Henry always ate more than anyone else.

Henry had become a quiet leader. He was always "up" and came ready to play. He was a "happy-go-lucky" guy and liked to have fun on the ice. Training was intensive. Henry liked to relax over a Harvey Wallbanger at the Burnsville Bowl.

pre-season

Murray had a rigorous schedule for the fledgling Olympians. They started out by beating the Cleveland Barons of the American Hockey League. Murray didn't sigh in relief; instead, he was reviewing the lines in his head, wondering if they were right.

On the personal scene Henry became a father. Baby Tara was born in Minneapolis on December 5, 1971.

They played Omaha again. Murray shuddered at the thought of facing them after last year, but knew the players needed this type of team to toughen them up. Omaha was waiting to pounce on the U.S. National players, and, less than a minute into the game, the Omaha intimidation began. Murray's Team was ready. Frank Sanders stood up to Vickers and cut him so badly that Vickers had to leave the ice. Minutes later, the U.S. team's nail-tough Dale Smedsmo, from Roseau, went at it with Omaha's Durbano. The fight lasted five minutes and Smedsmo was winning...until he was butted by Durbano's head and knocked down. Then Tim Sheehy won a fight. The Omaha coach was seething at the fate of his tough players and told Murray that the Omaha team wouldn't play any U.S. National Teams again ...particularly if Dale Smedsmo were on them. The Olympians beat Omaha that night and also the next match, when Henry scored in the last minute of the game to break a 4-4 tie. By Christmas, Murray's team had twenty-six wins, five losses and three ties, in playing minor-pro and college teams.

In Bemidji, Henry was late for the game against Bemidji State. Murray was furious. Henry said, "I thought it was half an hour later." Murray, fuming, retorted, "Don't think. From now on, I do all the thinking." Lyle Kvarnlov, Henry's old Warroad high school buddy, played for Bemidji. The Olympic team was dominating 10-0. There was a whistle. Lyle, going out for his shift, said to his teammate, "I'm going to take the puck away from Boucha." His teammate laughed, "Sure, Lyle." Henry snapped the puck and ripped down the ice with it. The clock was ticking off. He saw Lyle in the corner, and their eyes met; Henry's were twinkling. Henry flash-flipped the puck backhand across to his old friend Lyle's stick, just as the buzzer went off, an act of friendship Lyle never forgot.

At a game in Fargo, North Dakota, defensive dynamo Wally Olds, from tiny Baudette, Minnesota, went dashing into the zone in the corner. As he was leaning, reaching for the puck, he was bumped and went flying through the air toward a steel post that held the chicken wire in place. Wally managed to move his head out of the post's way but hit it full force with his collarbone, then landed flat on his back on the ice. Murray was irritated that Wally broke his collarbone. Doc insisted that the doctors put him in a full body cast so he would heal faster. Wally was back in the line-up the fourth weekend.

In Boston, after they played Harvard, Huffer got drunk. Murray was furious and said, "You're off the team." Huffer replied, "Screw you." Murray said, "You're on the 8:00 flight -- a.m.!" Huffer said, "If I'm leaving it's on the noon flight!" The next day a sober Huffer panicked. Murray gave him another chance. In the game that night, Huffer speared a guy and got thrown out of the game in the first period. Murray said, "You've got a hell of a streak going." That same night, Charlie Brown felt he could have played better and was afraid he would be sent back to Vietnam. Distraught, he went to his room and cried.

Russians

Murray's Team played the phenomenal Russian Red Army in five exhibition games. The Red Army knew how to play hockey better than anyone in the world. They even beat Team Canada, comprised of pro Canadian players. The Russians, pound for pound, were the strongest athletes in the world and were a machine that played together for years. They were cool, professional, hard-core, talented players.

The first time the teams sparred, in the Met Center, the Reds speared them on the backs of their legs and ankles. They hammered them, abused them, slashed them and were so skilled they did all this without the referees catching them. If the U.S. did anything to the Russians, they wouldn't retaliate. The cagey

Russians let the other team get the penalty. They lived for the power play; let the other team get frustrated was Tarasov's motto. The Russians were at their greatest provoking the high-strung Americans. These men operated as an awesome engine and were respected by everyone in the hockey world.

In one of these games, the U.S. boy-team was being shellacked by the Russian man-team. Henry was mad and spoiling for a fight and had been stirring it up with the Russians all night, nipping at their heels like a wolf pup. The Russians haughtily ignored him, but Henry wanted to use his battle-skills. Everything came to a head in an incident with Huffer in the net holding his stick straight out. (Huffer could be a dirty little player.) A Russian skated straight into Huffer's stick and screamed that Huffer had speared him. The mad Russian and Huffer went at it in a grand melee in front of the net. Each of them was handed a penalty.

The game continued, four on four, and then another deal broke out on the ice involving Henry. He dropped his stick and gloves to fight a Russian. The Russian, no fool, dropped his gloves faster. Quicker than a flashbulb-flash, his big Russian hands clamped like steel grips around Henry's arms. Henry couldn't move. The Russian, in full control of the situation with Henry locked down, looked to his bench with his eyebrows slightly raised. His coach gave a slight nod, and the Russian let go of Henry -- just as the Russian that was in the box with Huffer, jumped out of the penalty box and sucker-punched Henry in the side with one punch and socked him in the nose, breaking it, with another. The next thing Henry knew he was lying on the ice looking at the lights. And the *next* thing he knew he *and* Huffer were thrown out of the game. During period break the other players teased Henry. "Boy you really had *him* running!" Henry laughed at himself. "I never expected that!" he said.

Tom Mellor came racing off the ice toward the bench for a change-up. A Russian skater was standing alone. Mellor saw his chance to splat the Russian and make a name for himself. The Russian ducked: Mellor went diving over him, doing a humiliating belly flop. The cool Russian straightened up and watched disdainfully as Mellor slid across the ice on his stomach.

Before the U.S. – U.S.S.R. World Tournament game in Colorado Springs, right after Christmas, McGlynn and Mellor took a piece of paper and crunched it up like a microphone and did a *Mission Impossible* scenario to break the somber mood. It did the trick for awhile – until the team went out onto the ice.

The Red Army was doing somersaults and passing the puck in the air with their sticks. The Russian goaltender did a back flip over the net. They were doing incredible things with the puck. The U.S. Olympians just stood and watched in awe. The game started, and Olds got a shot from inside the blue line and scored. Then Sanders got one. The U.S. was actually ahead 2-0. Then the Russians put on the steam and scored 13 goals in a row. One would have sworn the ice was tilted toward the U.S. net.

The Russians beat the United States five out of the five exhibition games, but the experience the U.S. team gleaned from those games was invaluable in preparing for the Olympics.

Czechs

The next evening, after the loss to the Russians in the World Tournament in Colorado, the U.S. played the favored Czechs in an exciting seesaw contest. Henry was the leading game-scorer with four points. He scored two: one fired into the top left corner, textbook style, and the other belted straight in off a perfect pass from Olds. He and Olds later assisted Ahern, and Henry assisted Bader for the last U.S. goal. The U.S. came out the victor 7-5. Goalie Tim Regan turned in a stellar performance.

the final team

The final team Murray chose was the youngest Olympic hockey team ever assembled by the U.S. Three of the four youngest players on the 1972 Olympic hockey teams were from the U.S.; the other was a nineteen-year-old goalie from the Soviet Union.

The eight players returning from the '71 U.S. National Team were: Henry, Huffer Christianson, Tim Sheehy, Charlie Brown, Kevin Ahern, Tom Mellor, Dick McGlynn, and Jim McElmury.

McGlynn, in the Army and waiting for orders to be on loan from the Army to the Olympic team, was tearing his hair out. Those orders hadn't come. He called Murray and was told Murray was in Russia. He called Hal and was informed that Hal was in Sweden. He, an Army Private First Class, called the Pentagon! His unit was getting ready to ship out and he had his orders that said RVN (Republic of Vietnam) on them. Finally, thirty-six hours before he was scheduled to leave for Vietnam, his new orders came. McGlynn watched the boys he knew riding off in yellow buses, many of them his friends, to go to Vietnam as he rode off in a limo to catch a plane for the Olympics.

To the veterans, Murray added thirty-year-old Ron "Daddy" Naslund, who worried he was washed-up, and was surprised he made the team, and Dale Smedsmo, the tall, menacing defenseman from Roseau who played against Henry in high school and who played with Bemidji State now.

Stu Irving was called back from the Vietnam war. He had taken his hockey stick and pucks with him to the Mekong Delta and had kept up his game by shooting pucks into sandbags in the battle zone. He probably worked harder than anyone to make the team so he wouldn't have to go back to the war.

Murray took on Robbie Ftorek, a small, colorful 135-pound decisive competitor who played like a coiled spring. Robbie was a great playmaker and he was slippery and could slide sideways past the body checks of the big guys. He was an unbending perfectionist and gave no leeway for not doing one's best. Once, in high school, he forgot one of his shin guards. Instead of telling the coach, who would have had one of the lesser players sit so Robbie could use his leg pads, he wrapped three towels around his shins. When Dick McGlynn asked him what he did when someone took a shot at him Ftorek said, "It was easy. I lifted my leg." Later, when he played in the NHL, he became the first American player to be named NHL MVP. (Later in life, the story goes, as coach for the L.A. Kings, he benched Gretzky when he didn't think he was performing to his highest – the story goes on to say he was fired for this! Another anecdote is that he once had another player take a penalty shot instead of Gretzky, angering the crowd who had come to see the Great One play.)

Goaltender Pete Sears had driven to Minnesota with his wife and baby. He was penniless and got a job driving a forklift during tryouts. When Murray didn't say anything to him, he assumed Murray hadn't noticed him, so he drove all the way back home to New York with his wife and baby. When he got home Murray called and asked him where he was! Pete drove back across country – alone this time! When Murray told him he made the team he went to his room and cried. He was a back-up goalie, but was a team guy and always upbeat and supportive of the team. Pete became Henry's best friend on the team.

Tim Sheehy was in the Army but had been assigned to being a sports announcer on the Army radio. He was a talented winger and a much-touted Minnesota player: big, strong and fast.

"Cubby" Mellor was so excited to be on this team that when

he got into the game for the first time he got his stick stuck and fell out of the box -- splat onto the ice.

Three University of Minnesota veterans were added to the team: tried and true Wally Olds, "the smart one"; Edina's Bruce McIntosh; and big, reliable Gopher Captain, Frank Sanders, who would be a defensive rock.

Mike Curran, because of the fallout with Murray over his knee injury, did not try out. After the International Tournament in Switzerland he had knee surgery and had recovered nicely. Being without Curran was the one spot the team separated from Murray on. Curran could be an ornery son-of-a-bitch and Murray could be stubborn. But skating in the Olympics was the crest that Henry, and every other amateur hockey player, wanted to ride. They wanted to ride it with the best goalie possible...and in their minds that goalie was Curran and they wanted him to ride it with them. So, on the backtrack, a melodrama was being played out between Murray and the team concerning Lefty Curran. The team members were fighting for him. They needed him. Murray relented and asked Mike Curran to join the team two weeks before they left. Curran, stubborn to the end, said he would play if Murray would put personal feeling aside and let last year go. Murray said, "O.K. Let's go for it." The team felt confidence with Curran. He was the last factor needed to complete the complicated equation. Lefty Curran became the backbone of the team.

Tom Mellor and McGlynn, Easteners, were the team clowns who provided the much-needed comedy.

Tim Regan went as third goalie, but left midway through the games to go back and play for his college in their playoffs.

Henry, now twenty, was filling out. He was a highly skilled player, a flawless skater, a fluid stick handler and had a great shot. He could do things with the puck no one else on the U.S. team could do as a result of his days, weeks, months and hours on the Warroad River. He was strong, had great potential and had a quiet humility to go with it. He was physical, possessed a unaffected confidence, had great hands, and shot the puck like the Europeans. In 1972 as he started out for the 11th Olympiad in Japan's scenic, snowy north country in the city of Sapporo -- and the first Olympics ever hosted in Asia -- to represent the U.S. in ice hockey, he had the world by the tail.

Everything was going extremely well. Murray felt he had a terrific balance on his team. He had a solid core from last year, quick forwards and defensive strength.

Dale Smedsmo, the sheer tower of strength and intimidation from Roseau, had gone back to Bemidji and was doing a balancing act, playing with the college hockey team, taking the required classes at Bemidji State, and playing pre-season games with the Olympic team. Then the call came that Smedsmo had separated his shoulder in a game in Bemidji and would not be able to make the trip. For Murray it was a bad-luck setback. For Smedsmo, this tough and talented player, it was a personal catastrophe. He couldn't go to the Olympics, a goal he had worked for his entire hockey life. It took the athlete a year to get over it. Sixteen-year-old Mark Howe, son of former Detroit Red Wings superstar Gordie Howe, was added at the last minute.

Murray collected his team together and said, "We have twenty egos on this team. We will have problems. Please work it out. I feel if we do we will have a chance at a medal."

Murray's "super, super hockey team"

The U.S. hockey team that boarded the plane for the Olympics in Sapporo, was ranked on the bottom of the pile. The expectation for this scruffy team, according to the sportswriters and critics, was grim. They were shown no mercy.

The sportswriters and critics had forgotten to look into the hearts of these gifted American players. They didn't see how hard the kids worked off and on. They didn't look to see the invisible and unbelievable chemistry that banded these players together. Unnoted by them, the team members were sparks from the same fireworks. They were an optimistic group who liked and respected each other, and they were setting out with winning on their minds. The new Olympians were going as a lunch bucket team, working stiffs who never gave up even when they had been "spanked real bad" in pre-Olympic games. They were a tough group who didn't shy away from pain and hard work.

This courageous team, who defined perfectly what Olympians were supposed to be, was well aware of the job ahead of them. As with anyone destined for greatness, they sensed the destruction of listening to anything other than the whispers of winning and hope within themselves. The twelve teams were seeded according to how they had placed in Worlds the year before. The U.S. was seeded 6th because of last year's record.

The entire Olympic team gathered in Denver to fly together. Murray was informed that Doc Nagobads had been replaced by another doctor. The ever-loyal Murray said his team wouldn't get on the plane without Doc. Doc was signed on as a "cook" and the relieved group boarded the plane with him. The plane stopped at Seattle and then on to Anchorage, where it had a flat tire. When they reached Sapporo, a huge snowstorm prevented them from landing, so it was on to Tokyo. That night Wally Olds was watching tv and told his roommate to stop jumping on the bed. The roommate wasn't jumping on the bed...what Olds felt was the tremors from an earthquake. That same night Sanders roomed with Curran. Curran jumped up in the middle of the night and started making phantom saves in his sleep. It was the last time Sanders roomed with Curran. Sanders felt Lefty had had too many high hard ones!

The next day the Olympic entourage flew back to Sapporo and landed in a wonderland of deep snowfall. They were issued badges and passes and skated a practice. Then, in their rooms at Olympic Village, they jumped from their windows onto the colossal snow banks. It's a wonder their legs weren't broken. After that, they lounged in the Japanese ion-enzyme baths dressed in Pepto-Bismol pink paper jockey shorts.

Tokyo

The next day the hockey team flew back to Tokyo to play two exhibition games: Poland and the Czechs. Except for Murray fretting about lines, everything was going fine in the Polish game until the brawl in the second period. Andrej Szozepaniec from Poland speared Irving, resulting in five-minute majors for their clash. The Polish goalie, Walere Kosyl, kept entering the fray; it was Curran's job to keep him out. Curran threw Kosyl over the boards. Both goalies, Curran and Kosyl, were given ten-minute misconduct penalties. Players from both teams were swinging sticks viciously. Ahern and Sarner mixed it up; the referees tried to kick them both out of the Olympic games. They each had to go before the disciplinary committee, but Murray won the battle by saying that this was just an exhibition game, not the Olympics. (The U.S. won the game.)

Before the Czech game Sheehy, McGlynn, McIntosh and Henry went to Yokohama to the Army base to buy electronic equipment at the low prices the PX offered. Mac, who was not in the service, had to wait outside the gates. They bought Samsui speakers, cameras and electrical equipment, and were excited about their purchases. On the way back to the hotel the train screeched and gripped to a stop; the doors banged open and slammed closed, rocking the train. The boys were cringing at each jar for fear their precious acquisitions would be ruined. After they had gone quite a ways one of the guys realized they had gotten on the wrong train and were going the wrong way. Time was wasting and with churns in their stomachs about being late for the bus to the game, the boys gathered their purchases and got off the train as soon as they could. The wait for the train going back the other way seemed forever. Again, their precious cargo was abused by the jarring train. By now the boys were getting very nervous. It was getting late and they had a game to play.

By the time the seriously worried boys got back to the hotel the team wasn't there. The bus that took the team was gone. It had left for the rink without them. Now it was clear they were in deep trouble. To make matters worse there were several rinks in Tokyo and they had no idea which rink this game was being played in. They managed to find a taxi driver who turned out to be a maniac. He took a guess and got them to the right rink.

The besieged boys' problems weren't over. The teams went into the rink as a group and were admitted to the rink on a group pass. Henry and his renegade teammates had no ice rink pass. When they got to the door the attendant wouldn't let them in. They finally convinced him to locate the U.S. team coach.

By the time Murray was located, and much to their horror, the U.S. team was already on ice for warm-ups. Murray was mad as hell, waving his arms, yelling and kicking garbage cans. The boys got dressed to Murray's wrath.

During the game Murray was still going at it to Buddy about the lines. Buddy just sighed and listened. Murray's team lost the game 4-1, but Curran learned from the game, and felt they could beat the Czechs in the next contest. This was their final exhibition game and they were ready to take on the world.

parade

The parade of the Olympic athletes to officially start the games was spectacular. However, it was near disaster for the U.S. team, who were provided boots with *slick* leather soles...which slipped on the snow and ice...downing the athletes. In the last minute, *Operation Rubber* (attaching rubber to the bottom of the athletes' boots) was hastily instituted.

It was a proud U.S. hockey team that marched, securely on their new rubber soles, into Makomanai Stadium in their long navy blue leather coats: 50,000 people attended, including the Emperor of Japan. Henry was so excited he had bubbles in his stomach. The backdrop was the beautiful snow-clad mountains of Hokkaido. Flags flew on poles around the outside of the stadium. It was colorful and it was memorable for everyone there.

the qualifier

The first game was the qualifier against Switzerland on February 4th, 1972 (3:00 a.m. Minneapolis time). Henry and his roommate, Pete Sears, went for a bowl of chili before the game. They talked about the opposing players on the Swiss team. Henry never let up on preparing for games. The U.S. was not expected to win.

When the game started the hype was on. Emperor Hirohito was there, along with a capacity crowd. The outcome was simple: the winner went on to play in the Olympics, the loser did not.

Murray was, as usual, ruminating aloud to Hal about the lines. The players, including Curran, were nervous. In the second period, the Swiss goalie, Rigolet, made 26 saves, and in the third period the score was tied 3-3. Murray was going nuts and the players were sweating. It was then that Stu Irving got a hold of the puck and came whipping around the net with it, intent on scoring. He wrapped the net and stuffed the puck behind the Swiss goalie to break the tie. Now, with the U.S. in the lead by one point, it was Curran's turn to be nervous. If he could protect the goal his team would play in the Olympics. He put everything he had into it and did not let the Swiss score. The game belonged to the U.S. The celebration was on.

In the end the U.S. outshot the Swiss. A hot Rigolet had made 59 saves in the game, but Curran held the Swiss when it mattered...and Stu Irving, the boy fresh from the battlefields of Vietnam, made the most important goal of his life.

1st game Swedes (L)

The first official U.S. Olympic game was against Sweden. The Swedes had played an earlier qualifying game than the U.S. and had consequently gotten more rest between their game than the U.S. Sweden was ranked the second best team in the tournament, behind Russia, and had even tied the Russians once. Sweden was a great team with great athletes.

This was a tough game for the U.S. players because they scored two perfectly good goals that the Communist referee disallowed. On the first unapproved goal, the referee said that Nasland preceded Nalund into the net. This was not the case. On the second refused goal, the same referee said that Ftorek's stick was in the crease. Ftorek and Irving were right in front of the net and Nasland slid the puck across the crease. Robbie slapped it in. It was touch-bang play. You don't make that call!

Every time a U.S. player would so much as touch a Swedish player, the Swede would take a dive. The U.S. kept getting penalties and the Swedes kept scoring on the power play! Then the ornery Hedberg would skate by the bench waving his arm to rub it in to the Americans, which drove the U.S. team up a wall. The score was 5-1 Sweden, but should have been 5-3.

***

more history for those who want to know

Off this Swedish team were the first four Swedish players to become established in the NHL: Bjorge Salming, Ulf Nilsson, Anders Hedberg, and Inger Hammarstrom. They were impressively fast skaters. The Swedes had tied the Russians with 3 goals in the 3rd but they were beaten by the Czechs and Finns. Then the Czechs beat the Finns.

***

2nd game Czechs (W)

The third-ranked Czechs were favored to beat the U.S. team. Curran was always a good goalie, usually a great goalie and sometimes an off-the-charts phenomenal goalie. That's what he was in the Czech game. There was a lot of pressure to win and Curran gave it all he had. Valclav Nedomansky, who later played for the Detroit Red Wings, dominated forward play. He hammered Lefty the entire game. The Czechs kept coming in and pulling Curran one way, then sliding the puck across to the other side for one-timers. Curran "lit it up" becoming an acrobat, stopping all but one...a rammed shot from close range by Eduard Novak, from the stick of Pospisil -- the Czech Captain -- in the first period. They were both from Klando, Jaromir Jagr's, the Pittsburgh Penguins premier player's, hometown. Huffer scored in the last three minutes of the first period (with the Czechs two men short) on a loose puck scramble in front of the net.

Henry got a stupid retaliation penalty. Murray was furious. After his stint in the box, Henry tried to sneak back to the bench to avoid Murray, but Murray noticed him all right and was all over him. Henry's line made up for his penalty and scored in the second period. Buoyed up by Curran's play, McElmury shot from the blue line and Sarner deflected it past Czech goalie, Jiri Holeck. Then, with forty seconds left, Sanders blasted in a forty foot shot.

In the third period, Pospisil shot from the point to the left corner of Lefty's net...an incredible arrow, long and low. His arm was up in triumph as Lefty's toe made the save. The furious Czech broke his stick on the ice in anger.

The U.S. was outshot 52-23 in the game, but because of Curran's intense concentration, the U.S. won, chalking up a 5-1 upset victory. Lefty was the big hero. The announcer, Curt Gowdy, was going wild. He just couldn't believe the performance Lefty was giving. Curran had a swaggering "come on and shoot" mentality and felt he could stop the world. The defense had kept the puck from getting close to the net and Lefty said later that the long shots he saved were "the kind that made a goalie look good." The play was breathtaking: the sort of game that Olympics are made of. After the game, Murray said to Buddy, "Do you think the lines are O.K.?" An incredulous Buddy looked at Murray and said wearily, "Forget it, Murray. Let's have another drink."

***

stats to date for the curious

Sweden and Russia were tied for 1st place. Each had a victory and a tie. The Czechs, Finns and U.S. were tied. Each had one victory and one loss. Poland had two losses.

***

3rd game Russians (L)

The time had come to play the powerful CCCP: The Russian Red Army. Mihilov (who later became the Russian Red Army coach), Davidoff (who, curiously, could speak English), Petrov, Kharmolov, and Firsov were heralded the best players on the Russian team...and in the tournament. They were all creative players and magnificent to watch. Petrov could stop a slap shot with his stick. One time the referee missed a puck that was shot over to him for a face-off. Petrov, standing behind the referee, caught it on his stick and tossed it back to the referee. The crowd loved it.

There were few U.S. fans at the arena in far-away Sapporo; the faces were mostly Japanese. The disciplined Americans didn't let the lack of fans get in their way. They were up for the game and wanted to show what the U.S. could do against these uncompromising, professional men.

Before the game Murray said to Stu, "Can you shadow Kharmolov, Stu?" The eager Stu answered, "I'll sure try." Stu was trying to do his part, shadowing Kharmolov and zestfully doing everything else he could do to stop the Russians. He went into the corner, checking large Russian #4. Russian #4 was growing tired of Stu; he butt-ended Irving in the mouth to get him off his back. Stu took six stitches over this one.

Henry had many chances for goals in the first period, but the goalie was always ahead of him. Then Henry got a rebound and a clear shot on goal. He whammed the puck toward the net and tossed his hand in the air in triumph – just as Kharmolov dove in the path of the puck, stopping it with his head.

Frank Sanders intercepted a Russian pass, only to see it ricochet off his stick, past Curran into his own net. He made up for it, scoring on a pass from Sheehy early in the third.

The game was played as tightly and tough as sparring Elk males...the best contest the U.S. had against the Soviet Union that year. Curran, and his heroics, had a great game with 50 saves, but, at the end the board read: Russians 7, Americans 2. "Daddy" Naslund put in the second goal. The American hockey fans, at home, were not treated to the incredible battle Murray's "super, super hockey team" waged against the mighty Russian Red Army.

4th Game Finns (W)

The Czech game had been Curran's. The next game, against the Finns, was Henry's. Everyone else was getting tired, but Henry was pumped for this game. He won the first face-off and passed to his right wing, Sarner, who streaked for the net. Sarner shot from about 30' out and the puck bounced loudly against the inside right post...and just as quickly went out again. The referee signaled a goal. Jorma Valtonen, the goalie, hotly protested the goal but to no avail. Henry scored two of his own in the first period. He was all over the ice. The final score was 4-1, U.S. Murray said, "The boys didn't have their legs tonight, they played with their hearts."

5th game Poles (W)

In the game against the Poles the U.S. was ahead 6-1 and feeling their oats. Feliks Goralczyk of Poland was awarded a penalty shot. Goralczyk swept in to the left of Curran, who came out and forced him to shoot wide to the right. Bab Nadin, a Canadian referee, ruled that Curran had come out of the goal crease too soon and awarded Goralczyk another shot. The Pole responded by coming in to Curran's right and shooting wide again. Curran picked up the puck and said, "Do they get another one?" The referee said, "No," but the guys from the U.S. bench, really into this by now, were yelling, "Give him another one!" or "Hey! Try a third time!"

silver

The games were over for the U.S. Murray's Team had played extremely well, and the boys and Murray were proud with their three win, two loss record. There were two games left to be played -- the Finns against the Swedes, and the Russians vs. the Czechs. It was expected that the Swedes would beat the Finns.

The U.S. Team attended the Finn-Swede game as a group and when the Finns upset Sweden the boys realized they had a medal secured. The Silver Medal was theirs if the Russians beat the Czechs...if the Czechs won the U.S. would get the Bronze. The entire team went to the U.S.S.R. – Czechoslovakia game clad in white sweaters. They, except for Ftorek*, cheered for the Russians and when Russia won, the U.S. team had acquired a Silver Medal for the Red, White and Blue. Murray's dream had been realized; his trilogy was over. He had won a medal for the U.S. -- the first hockey medal for the U.S. in twelve years. His Olympic team came in second to the greatest Russian team ever -- and above the fiery Swedes.

Lefty Curran called it a "storybook ending", but his heroics

---

*Ftorek cheered for the Czechs because: the U.S. already had a medal. It would have been a Bronze medal if the Czechs had won. He didn't feel it was important whether the U.S. got a Bronze or Silver medal but he felt if the Czech team won Curran would have a chance of being selected to the All-World team.

were instrumental in writing the book that put the Silver around their necks.

For the mothers, fathers, wives, girlfriends, grandparents, brothers, sisters, fans, friends, and relatives at home there was bitter disappointment: the cameras were turned off minutes before the U.S. received their medal. The broadcast was interrupted because it was Northern Ireland's Bloody Sunday.

The coverage of the games had been pathetic back home. The games were played in the middle of the night by U.S. clocks and forgotten by the reporters the next day. Americans were very unhappy that an under-matched team of amateurs had to be sent to do battle against Eastern Bloc athletic wage earners ...amateurs in name only...whose hockey skills garnered them Army commissions. As the U.S. team had come in last place the year before at the International Competition in Switzerland, no one expected much. So, coming in second in these Olympics was a giant boost to the American morale: it proved that amateur players *could* make a fantastic world showing.

There was a lot of excitement in the Armed Forces for the games. In Vietnam, the Army radio broadcast the game and gave the soldiers a thrilling account. It meant a lot to the boys who needed that uplift from the home front. Kent LeMoine, Henry's high school hockey rival from Thief River Falls, stationed in the Army in Korea, proudly told his buddies he had played against Henry in high school.

On a personal level, Henry had fulfilled the trilogy and was ready for the pros.

aftermath

The Olympic torch was returned to the sun. Eight Japanese soldiers carried the Olympic flag out and Avery Brundage declared the games over in the presence of Crown Prince Akihito.

Coming home in the plane from Japan, players were talking excitedly on the phone. The NHL draft was going on and everyone was yelling where everyone else was going in the draft. President Nixon sent a telegram. The governor of Minnesota, Wendy Anderson, invited them to the Governor's Mansion (but never followed through). But it was exciting then because they thought they were going to the Governor's Mansion! The players wore their medals when they disembarked the plane in Minneapolis.

After the Olympics, Murray set up a deal to play an exhibition game in Las Vegas with the Las Vegas Outlaws. The players stayed at Ralph Engelstad's Imperial Palace. (Ralph was from Thief River Falls, Minnesota, and had played hockey himself many years earlier, tending goal in the first Minnesota State High School Tournament in 1945.) After the second period, Ralph came into the locker room to offer each player $100.00 to keep the score down. It was all in good fun and the players enjoyed a much deserved vacation.

Two games were played but Henry left for Detroit and the NHL Red Wings before the second game. It all happened so fast there were no formal goodbyes. After the second game the team sort of drifted out of the locker room. There was never an official good-bye to each other and most of the players went home with an empty, unsatisfied feeling after the intense camaraderie they had shared. Henry went on to the busy life of the NHL, but his years with Murray and the National Teams had made a strong impact on him.

***

some more trivia for diehards

Henry Boucha was the #1 season scorer for the Olympic team. In the 1972 Olympics Charlie Brown and Wally Olds never had a goal scored against them. The U.S. got the medal because, even though they had tied with the Czechs for points, they had beaten the Czechs earlier in the tournament. Even the Sapporo Olympics weren't without incident. An Austrian ski star, Karl Schranz, was ousted from the games for taking money. A Spaniard, Fransisco Fernandez Ochoa, won the first winter Olympic medal ever for Spain (downhill skiing). The U.S. placed fifth overall in the Olympics.

PART V

RED WINGS

MISKWA NIGWIGON... "RED WING"
OJIBWAY

28

The "Big Show"

When Henry was ten years old there was a contest in Warroad. Whatever child sold the most candy would win a trip to Winnipeg to see the Toronto Maple Leafs play the Detroit Red Wings. Henry was determined to win that contest. He hustled like a beaver getting ready for a hard winter and sold candy door to door. He was a serious child, and who could say no to the big, eager eyes. Henry sold enough to win the contest.

The game was a thrilling experience for the youngster. The Red Wings trounced the Maple Leafs. It was then that Henry decided he would play for the Red Wings some day.

contract

Ned Harkness, general manager of the Red Wings, came to Las Vegas, where Henry was celebrating with the Silver Olympians, to meet with Henry. Glen Sonmor, who was now the coach of the WHA St. Paul Fighting Saints (Henry was their #1 draft choice) also called Henry and offered him money just to come and talk to him...before he made a final decision to sign with Detroit. Henry, who had wanted to play with the Detroit team since he was ten, was ready to sign with them. Henry and Harkness came to terms with a one-year contract and an option year. He was guaranteed to the "big club" the rest of the season. His signing bonus was $25,000 and his salary was $50,000 a year.

The upstart WHA (World Hockey Association) was causing panic in the NHL; some of their best players were defecting to the new league.

Debby and Henry had fought constantly in Las Vegas. He had hoped for a happy reunion and some peace, but that was not what was happening. He left Las Vegas and the Olympians and Murray, his coach for three years. Murray and the other players had become a family to him.

Henry and Debby flew to Detroit where they checked into the airport Ramada. Baby Tara had been left in Warroad with Debby's mother. The Red Wings were playing the New York Rangers at Madison Square Garden that night. Henry sat in the hotel room and watched the game on tv, hardly able to believe that he would be playing with these fabled men...including Alex Delvecchio, Marcel Dionne, and Red Berenson, the very next night in historic Olympia Stadium.

After a sleepless night Henry went to Olympia Stadium for a press conference and meeting with the coach, Johnny Wilson, who was a former Red Wing player. As he was walking down the hall corridor to Wilson's office he went by an open door. Sutherland, the player who was being sent down so that Henry could crack the line-up, was sitting there getting the news that he was no longer a Red Wing. This didn't make Henry very popular with the guy's friends on the Red Wings.

Henry got all new equipment and was issued #12. He wanted his old high school #16 but someone already had it. The team had a light pre-game skate and Henry skated with them.

Debby was sulking and didn't go to his first NHL game. That evening, trying to find the arena, Henry got lost in the strange city. Somehow the city looked different at night and disorientated him. He finally found the arena and then the attendant didn't want to let him in to park. He finally talked his way in. The attendant made him park way on the other side. By now Henry was very late so he sprinted across the dark lot so he could make it on time. When he got to the building the door guard had no intention of letting him by and stood firmly by his sacred door. Finally Henry talked him into phoning someone inside and Henry got the go ahead. By now he was half an hour late for his first NHL game.

The big moment had come. Henry would be realizing his childhood dream that he had dreamed on the obscure Warroad River as he practiced every move until it was perfect. He was playing in the NHL and for his favorite team, the mighty Detroit Red Wings. He went into the dressing room and was immediately awestruck. This sense of awe never left him the entire time he played in the NHL. It was a rush sitting there getting dressed with all the pros...the top guns...the best of the best. The tough guys did not welcome the upstart with open arms. It definitely was not a sorority social. Some were not happy a fellow skater had been replaced by Henry, but it was a job for all of them. Henry had to prove himself to be accepted.

When the team hit the ice for warm-ups Henry was really nervous. All the new equipment felt strange. #12 felt strange. The arena felt strange. The other players were strange. He hadn't skated for over a week because the Olympic hockey team had finished a couple of days before the Olympics were over. After that there was the flight back from Japan, then a few days in Las Vegas (you couldn't count the Las Vegas game as skating) and then there was the trip back east. Henry started skating around the ice with the others. Butterflies were lighting up his stomach. The house was packed. He circled like a planet held in place by the sun. The excitement, like the state high school tournament, waved in the air like a victorious flag. When the veteran Red Wings lined up on the blue line to shoot pucks at the goalie, Henry was too nervous and just kept skating around in circles. At twenty he was the youngest player on the Red Wings.

***

Henry was sitting on the bench watching the play. He hadn't been on the ice yet. The team was down by a couple of goals and Toronto was called for a two-minute minor. The coach looked down the bench and said to Henry, "You! You! Get out there on left wing." So his first shift in the NHL was on a power play. This experience was very similar to his first high school game, when Coach Grafstrom sent him in on the power play against Roseau when he was in the 8th grade. Only this time he was on a line with Mickey Redmond and Alex Delvecchio, who was in his twenty-third year in the pros.

Henry walked the play down into the Toronto end. The defense didn't see him. Mickey Redmond had the puck in the right corner. Henry was clear in the slot area and Redmond gave him a beautiful pass. Henry one-timed it. The ping sounded through the huge arena. The puck hit the pipe!

At the beginning of the second period the Red Wings were behind 4-0. Al Smith, the Red Wing goalie, was being bothered by a testy Toronto player who was staying in the crease every chance he got. Finally Smith had had it. He chased the player down the ice and jumped on the guy's back. The big brawl that followed was Henry's first taste of NHL fighting and his Jets training was invaluable. The fans were going nuts. Henry loved the roar of the crowd.

This hot-headed move by Smith turned out to be the turning point in the game. Everyone on Detroit rallied around, including the Wings' newest wing, Henry.

1st NHL goal

Henry was on the ice again. He wanted to contribute to this team and to belong. He was out with Alex Delvecchio and Mickey Redmond again. Henry was forechecking like crazy. The puck was free. Henry grabbed his chance and hit the puck toward the net. The obliging puck bounced like a smooth stone skipping on a glassy pond, effortlessly, over Toronto goalie, Jacque LaPlante, who was coming out for it. Score!

It was pretty impressive to score his first NHL goal in his first game. Now the score read 4 on the Toronto side and a precious 1 for the Red Wings. Toronto still had the lead, but the Detroit Red Wings were on the board and fired up. Henry had scored the goal that started the comeback.

In the end the Red Wings won the game by beating Toronto 5-4, in an old-fashioned cliff hanger, and just as he had in the little Warroad rink in 8th grade, Henry gained the respect of the players and the sophisticated NHL crowd very quickly.

***

After this game the team had a couple of days off. It had been a tremendous week for Henry. He had gotten back from the Japan Olympics and signed with the Red Wings. He had flown to Detroit, had a press conference, met his new coach and teammates, played his first game in the "Big Show" and scored. After the game he flew back to Minneapolis to pack up the furniture for the movers.

Henry was still in the service. He took a day off from practice and flew to Chicago to muster out of the Army (a six months early out...the Army was downsizing). Tom Kohl, a friend from the service, met him at the Chicago airport and took him where he needed to go. It took Henry all day to get mustered out. In total, Henry spent eighteen months in the service. That evening he was on a plane back to Detroit and very much a free man.

Henry and Debby got an expensive apartment in Detroit and hired a pricey interior designer to decorate it with upscale furniture. Debby hated Detroit from the beginning. She would stay a week, there were always the fights, and then she would fly home with the baby.

The team took a Western swing "road trip" by air. They went to L.A., Oakland, and Vancouver, Canada. On the flights all the players took up the back of the plane and gambled and drank heavily. Henry had never seen anything like it. On the National Teams there was the occassional opportunity to sneak behind Murray's back for a few drinks, and a few of the guys, but certainly not all, drank, but this was not the same. It was hard core. Henry, always wanting to get along and to belong, just went along with what everyone else was doing.

Once the team got to their destinations, they wouldn't play for a couple of days. The players rented limos and bar-hopped; Henry got his first taste of what these guys were like on the road. It was hard party. Not every player was like that, but most were. It was a party lifestyle. The Canadian players just grew up that way, having played in hockey clubs away from home since they were fourteen and fifteen years old. Home was the locker room.

Playing in the Forum in Montreal was one of the biggest thrills in Henry's life. The packed crowd had unbridled enthusiasm and loyalty for their team. The Forum itself was incredible. The history was there, plus it was continually being made. Ken Dryden was the goalie. Guy Lapoint, Henry Richard and Guy LaFleur were on the roster. They had won the Stanley Cup the previous year and were on the way to winning it this year – for the seventeenth time!

When they played the Blackhawks in wild and woolly Chicago, Bobby Hull scored his 49th and 50th goals against the Red Wings.

Henry played with the Red Wings the last nineteen games of the '71-'72 season. He had played well, but the team didn't make the playoffs, which was a disappointment because they were off by only 1 point. (In the early '70's there were only two divisions in the NHL; there are four now.)

summer of troubles

After the season, Henry drove home from Detroit. He told Debby he was going to stop in Minneapolis on the way back to see his brother, David, his old coach, Murray, and Hal Trumble. She didn't want him to and made a fuss about it. She told him to come straight to Warroad, but he felt he needed to stay in contact with these people. He had a strong bond with Murray and Hal after three seasons of playing for them. He wanted to thank them, and share his NHL experiences.

He called Murray to meet him for lunch and when they sat down Henry lit up a cigarette and ordered two Manhattans. Murray almost fell off his chair. He didn't know Henry drank or smoked. He also went to lunch with Hal Trumble, the manager of the U.S. teams.

When Henry got home to Warroad all his suitcases were on the front steps. He grabbed the suitcases and went to stay with his parents. Upset that Debby wouldn't see him or talk with him he packed up his car and headed to Minneapolis, left his car with David and flew to Idaho with his younger brother Eddie for a month with his older sister, Darlene.

After his visit with Darlene, he flew back to Minneapolis and drove to Detroit. (Eddie, who had been the back-up goalie when Henry was a senior in high school, went to Victoria, British Columbia to play junior hockey.) When Henry opened the door to his apartment, it was as bare as Old Mother Hubbard's shelf. Everything but his clothes were gone. He went to the bank. The bank manager came out and told him Debby had cleaned out the checking and savings account. Henry's own checks that he had written, assuming he had plenty of funds to cover them, had bounced. At just twenty-one he was financially wiped out. He had to make arrangements at the bank to get a loan. Then Debby went on a secret-to-Henry spending spree, charging a car and $25,000 more in clothes and various and sundry things. Henry got a call from the Red Wings' accountant that people from *Collections* were calling him. Henry was being sued for unpaid bills that he didn't even know he had. Training camp hadn't even started. Henry had to get an attorney in Detroit. The lawyer renegotiated Henry's contract and talked to the creditors and got Henry back on track. He also started divorce proceedings.

Henry placed an ad in the Warroad paper that he was not responsible for any debts other than his own.

Gordie Howe

Back in Detroit, a very kind, recently retired Red Wing player, Gordie Howe, who was now vice president of the club, took Henry under his wing. He gave Henry tips and pointers and got him making hospital visits, etc. Henry was amazed at how Gordie handled himself around children who were terminally ill. He simply tried to make a better day for them. They loved him. In August, Henry worked at Gordie's hockey school.

the decisions

So, Henry's first decision out of high school to play with the Canadian Jets, instead of going to the University of Minnesota, was indeed the right move. His three years on the U.S.A. team couldn't have been a better place to mature at his craft. He was a much stronger, tougher and technically better player because of juniors and nationals.

His incredibly destructive choice -- marriage to Debby -- was a disaster to him in every way. *Financially* she ruined him and drove him far, far down the rabbit hole. *Emotionally,* in Debby, he never had anyone to talk to and be supportive of him: it was quite the opposite – it was always the push away from center, always keeping him on the brink. *Spiritually* there was no thread at all. *Physically* she would deprive him of sleep and claw at him when she was angry. *Intellectually...*there was no intellectually. Henry was a sensitive person. He cared about others. He valued life. He needed and he yearned for the depth of a worthwhile personal relationship.

Henry was living a nadir – zenith life. He was in the syrup of a divorce that was necessary because of a torturous married life, but he had hit the heights in his career. He liked playing for the Red Wings. He liked Detroit. He liked the coach and playing the game with and against the best. He liked the amenities afforded the sports figure. He was looking forward to next season with the Red Wings and the glitter of the NHL he had worked so hard to be part of.

29

Chief

It is true that Henry was a multi-talented, seasoned athlete when he reported to the Red Wing training camp in the fall of 1972 for preparation of the '72 –'73 season. There was no doubt in the mind of the hockey world that Henry Boucha was on the brink of a grand and glorious career. He had it all. Talent. Speed. Moves. The ability to see the ice. The rocket shot. Skating and plays that produced electricity in the crowd. A toughness, and at the same time, a beauty. Mystical. Shrewd. Boucha was magic.

***

Training camp was held in Ft. Huron, Michigan. The Detroit Red Wings, London Lions, Tidewater Wings, a team in Ft. Huron, and a team in Johnstown, Pennsylvania, were all owned by the Red Wings and held their tryouts for all the clubs at the same place and at the same time. There were a ton of players trying out for all the levels.

The Red Wing tryouts were brutal. Two ice times were held a day: a grueling two-hour session in the morning and another in the afternoon. Earl Anderson, an old high school rival from Roseau, came to try out. Earl, and everyone else, was wiped out after each session and ready to crawl to the dorms for a nap between sessions and a long, recuperative night's sleep after the second session. Henry accosted Earl, and everyone else, and said, "Hey, I know some great places in Detroit (90 miles away). Let's go party." Earl had to plead fatigue as he watched Henry bounding off for his car, alone, like he had been a spectator at the tryout instead of the blazing star. In the morning, Henry would come back to camp after a night of partying. He would stretch out on the benches and get an hour or so nap then hit the ice and be the best player out there.

Henry had fun at camp. He roomed with Delvecchio, partied at night and played golf with the Red Wing veterans in the afternoon break.

***

As it was true that Henry was Zeus on ice, his personal life was broken. Being so busy and partying was a cover-up for these problems, but no one knew it then.

Henry loved being with people. He always had – since his earliest faint impressions of the happy visitors to the snug little cabin on the peaceful shores of Buffalo Bay, embraced by his large and larger extended family and later at the little house in Warroad with all the drop-ins. He was away from the sheltering arms of his family, the U.S. teams, and the Jets. He was the youngest player on the Red Wings, but it was a sink or swim situation. The other players didn't give a rip about the emotional well-being of their fellow players, no matter what their age was. The Red Wings were not the fun-loving, rather naïve "brothers" the National Team players had been. Murray made sure his players were nurtured: he, Hal and Doc watched over them and cared about them. Henry's high school coaches had all been the same way. The Jets were all guys about the same age and shared a camaraderie like kids at camp. Henry was used to being emotionally nourished, even adulated, on his career level.

The Red Wings, as an organization, had no help for players. No orientation when you got there. No support group. No help in how to act or what to say at hospitals where kids were dying. No help in how to give a speech – and yet they were called on to speak at many civic functions. No cap on the drinking and partying. There was no one to be concerned. That was a tough adjustment for Henry. The players were hard core (and sometimes crass) men. The surface of playing in the NHL was bright and shiny (and he did love that part), but underneath the glitter was a void: a deadness like a shimmering lake that looks good from far off but when you get there it is dead with no fish, no vegetation. It was, at best, unsettling. There was no point to grab on to and no light to see where one was headed in the long haul.

His parents loved him but they weren't part of his jet-set life-style and continent-hopping. They couldn't help him in his new world. They couldn't be expected to understand. He was severed from them by what they and Henry wanted him to be. An ice god. The god knew more than his parents – and less – but at this place in his life he thought he knew more.

The marriage was over. His baby was withheld from him, and worse, Debby rarely let his parents, who desperately wanted to be part of her life, see little Tara. The divorce was not an easy move for him because of the baby but it was futile to go on and he couldn't have an economic and emotional repeat of last year...he was still paying off her spree and would be for all of the next season.

The '72-'73 season was Henry's rookie year. Johnny Wilson

was still the coach. After training camp, most of the team, including Henry, stayed at the Continental Hotel while they were looking for places to live. He rented a furnished house in Allen Park with some of the other players. He settled in, but didn't settle down. The nasty divorce and subsequent feeling like he was losing his daughter was shattering him emotionally. Not having people around who cared for the players as individuals was an adjustment he was not able to deal with.

The superstar, who appeared to the fans as if he had everything going for him, was hurting badly and no one knew it. His heart was not into the game. He was lonely and his personal problems created so much inner turmoil that concentrating on hockey became secondary...then he lost the concentration altogether. He started to self-destruct with drinking and partying. The team was on the road a lot and there was no one to talk to for help in getting his head straightened out. He just melded into the team and became what this society expected of him...losing an important part of his identity as he did so. Deep down inside him the soft Ojibway drums were trying to beat another rhythm, the one Alice had taught him, but, like he was in a dream-world...or the drums were...he couldn't get to them.

During the Western swing, he started not playing well, and was benched. Wilson talked to him in Oakland and told him he was sending him down to the American League to get in shape and jump-start him. Henry thought Wilson was wrong and felt belligerent about it. Wilson put him on a plane back to Detroit all by himself while his teammates carried on the road trip. Henry had never felt failure before. He felt like he had hit rock bottom. And, even more, he felt terrible and worried what his parents would think. He didn't want to shame them and, with that thought foremost in his mind, it jarred him to make the decision to work hard and get in shape and use being sent down as a stepping-stone, not as a gravestone. He was sent to the Tidewater Wings in Norfolk, Virginia.

It was while Henry was in Norfolk that the drums came out of the dream world and started beating within him. He found who he was. Career-wise, the Tidewater Wings were tonic for Henry. He played seven games with them, picked up assists and goals and got his confidence back. It was the best thing that could have happened to him.

It was also while Henry was in Norfolk that he stopped wearing his helmet. He scored the very first time he took it off and decided it was good luck not to wear it, so he discarded it.

At that time it was fashionable to have long hair. His long hair with sweat on it would fall into his eyes and the combination would mess up his contact lenses.

headbands and Indians

It was time for Henry to go back up to the Big Show. This time he was ready. He had faced himself and was ready to jump the hurdles and do what it took to be a force in the NHL, to concentrate on his game and to the give the Red Wings everything he could on, and off, the ice. He couldn't control what Debby did but he was ready to control what he did.

When Henry got back he didn't want to wear a helmet anymore and was talking to Tom Jafire, the Dearborn Ice Rink manager, about how to keep his hair out of his eyes. Tom walked into the tennis pro shop and came back with a couple of white headbands. The team was playing Pittsburgh at home and Henry decided to try the headband for the game. He combed his hair down and sprayed his hair. The guys razzed him because they thought he was jazzing up the Indian thing. When the coach came in for pre-game he asked Henry, "What's that?" Henry said it would keep the hair out of his eyes so the hair and sweat couldn't bother them. Games were being won and the team was in a good position, so Wilson let it go. Someone yelled "Hippie" when Henry hit the ice, but the notion was quickly replaced with "Indian" and then to "Chief."

The headbands did the trick in keeping the sweat and hair out of his eyes, so he kept wearing them. They became a trademark for him. A lot of people thought he was showcasing the *Indian thing* and that was the reason for them. Henry did get a lot of publicity over the headbands: the media jumped on it; the crowd jumped on it; the team organist jumped on it. Every time Henry hit the ice, the organist would play Indian music. The fans would go wild and stand and cheer. Even Montreal Canadians fans picked it up and would chant a warning in unison, "Bo Shaw! Habs on the Warpath," when the Red Wings played in Montreal. (The Habs was the nickname for the Montreal Canadians.)

Henry started marketing the headbands through the Red Wing pro shop and it was a fun thing for the fans. Players from other teams started making racial slurs, but Henry could deal with that.

On the flip side, the militant Native Americans called him Uncle Tomahawk – an Indian's Uncle Tom. It was a tough time for Native Americans who were fighting against a very real oppression. They were struggling for social justice that had been denied them for nearly five hundred years. These Indian peoples resented the war chant the Detroit organist played when Henry stepped on the ice. Further, they resented the headband. Most of all they resented that he wouldn't get involved and come aboard for their cause or comment on the Wounded Knee "incident" in South Dakota.

Henry didn't join with them because he didn't understand the social inequities at that time. His mother had never tried to make him a militaristic Indian. She had not bucked the social injustices the Anglo-American conquerors laid on the Native American because in isolated Warroad the small band wasn't aware of the broad scope of destruction to the Native Americans at the hands of the white man. She was not an activist and wanted her son to blend in.

Later in life Henry sought his roots, but at that time, when he was twenty-one and playing hockey for the Red Wings, he hadn't thought through what being a Native American was. He enjoyed the headband and the music and the response of the fans to his Indianness. Henry was connected to his Indian roots firmly by his mother, but like the flower of the rose reaching out and up he didn't understand the iris or the lily. He was trying to understand himself.

Henry started playing regularly again. The old fire was in him. He got 14 goals and 14 assists the last half of the season. January 23, 1973 he set the record for the fastest NHL goal after a game started. The game was against the Canadians in Montreal and was scored on Wayne Thomas in a nationally televised game at six seconds after the start of the game and broke the 1932 record of seven seconds by Charlie Conacher which had stood for forty-one years. Henry didn't know he had set the record until a tv interview at the end of the game.

Mike Lamey, of the Hockey Spectator, quoted Henry, "It happened so fast," was Boucha's understatement, "I found myself in front of the net with the puck. I didn't know what to do. The puck was bouncing and I shot a backhander. The puck fluttered and I don't think the goalie was expecting it."

Lyle Kvarnlov, who went on to play at Bemidji State, didn't realize how good Henry really was until he was watching Henry and the Red Wings play against the Bruins on tv. Bobby Orr had the puck. The Red Wings were two men short. Henry chased Bobby Orr and trapped him like a very smart wolf cornering a frightened deer. The crowd was going absolutely wild and cheering for Henry. Orr coughed up the puck and Henry received a standing ovation.

NBC televised the games and always wanted to talk to Henry. He was a media person's dream. The interviewers always walked right by the big guns, who had 40 goals a season, and headed straight to Henry. The prima-donnas were not happy about being snubbed, but Henry had gotten his life back and he was happy once again.

The fans loved Henry. He was a giving person. He would always patiently sign autographs outside the Detroit dressing room (he felt this went with the job) and was a favorite at the hospitals and at speaking engagements. Not all of the Red Wings would go out on the public relations jaunts but Henry always did. Gordie Howe, a very perceptive person, was a help to Henry in this area. He took Henry under his wing. In turn, Henry became a Big Brother to a nine-year-old boy who needed help and companionship. The last part of the season saw a new Henry Boucha, a take-charge person who was working out his problems and doing a very good job.

At the end of season play, the Red Wings finished in fifth place again...two points out. The team had such a strong nucleus that year. Henry thought the team was going places. But the record was not quite enough to go to the playoffs. It was a disappointing end to the season.

summer

After the season was over the team had a year-end party at a bar in Detroit. It was a nice time and goodbye for some, but Henry knew he was coming back for the '73-'74 season.

As soon as he could, he flew to Florida alone for some much needed R and R. He stayed at hotels and visited friends. He drove a rented car to Key West down the beautiful Florida Keys. It was a very relaxing vacation.

After that he went to Kentucky to visit Jack and Ruth Ploof from his Warroad high school days. During the Olympics, Henry had snuck Jack into the Olympic Village in Sapporo. Jack, who was working in Okinawa, came to see Henry. He took a bus to the Olympic Village. Henry came to the gate to meet Jack toting a USA jacket in a bag...Jack put the jacket on. They walked around to the back gate and Jack walked in. The guard assumed he was a hockey player along with Henry. Jack stayed with the athletes in their apartments and Henry got him meal tickets. This would never be able to be done now, because at the 1972 Summer Olympics, in Munich, Germany, eleven Israeli Olympians were killed. Ever since then, sadly and out of necessity, security has been very tight at Olympic Villages.

Henry flew back to Detroit and then boarded another flight to Bemidji, Minnesota, to speak to Indian student-athletes. His younger brother, Eddie, drove Henry's car back to Warroad from Detroit so Henry would have "wheels" during the summer months.

It was a hectic summer, but Henry was finally back on track financially, after paying off all Debby's charges, so the next year he would be able to have some of his hard-earned money for himself and to help his parents. He wanted to buy them a good home.

At the end of summer, it was back to Detroit for his own Henry Boucha Hockey School, held just before the Red Wings training camp. His "Little Brother" was included. Henry was very serious about his camp.

Jack Berry, *Detroit News*, quoted Henry in an interview at that time:

"I don't agree with the way a lot of hockey schools are fun. They're just a big rip-off. Players put their names on them and then they spend very little time with the kids or they're out partying the night before and aren't in shape and don't put anything into it.

These kids and their parents are paying good money and a lot of them are poor and it's a sacrifice for them to get the money together. I think they should get their money's worth."

***

Henry had pulled his life around the last half of the season. He was playing well and was a fan pleaser with his headbands and electrifying play. He was on the Advisory Board of American Indian Services that specialized in helping Indians in prison, was a "Big Brother," ran his own hockey school and was a favorite at the hospitals and as a speaker for the Red Wings. He was also taking two college classes.

Henry, the colorful player the fans called "Chief," was mentally and physically ready for the '73-'74 Red Wings season.

In 1973 Henry was on top of the heap of young NHL players and priming himself for a stellar career.

At the beginning of the season in an exhibition game, Dale Smedsmo, his old Roseau rival, played against Henry in a game at

Maple Leaf Gardens. Smedsmo was playing for the Maple Leafs. Henry was late for the game and the angry coach disciplined Henry by benching him -- except for penalty kills. Smedsmo watched in awe as his old rival, now surfaced as new rival, made two goals against the Maple Leafs, playing only on penalty kills! In Smedsmo's opinion, no one could carry Henry's skates at that point in his career. He made all the plays and didn't have to go to the corner.

The team was picked and Henry was ready. Each year representatives from the National Hockey League had meetings at the beginning of the season where the players were warned about the do's and don'ts of NHL hockey. They were told not to get involved with the Mafia, stay away from hookers, what to do if you're blackmailed, who to call if you got picked up in a bar, what to do if someone approached you to throw a game, etc. Players were also warned not to get involved in anything that would hinder the NHL reputation.

Johnny Wilson got fired during the summer (Henry felt he was one of the best coaches he had ever had) and Ted Gavin, from the Port Huron minor league team, came in as head coach for the Red Wing '73-'74 season. The older players had no respect for him, so there was a lot of tension and division from the beginning. There was no unity. Morale was bad. The team was not playing as a team. Henry was used for the penalty kill and power play and was racking up 40 minutes a game, so he had no complaints on a personal level. He was just trying to do his part for the team. The team wasn't winning. The older players would bitch and moan and were rude to Gavin. Henry felt it must have been hard on Ted Gavin, who was trying his hardest and who was such a fine coach.

One day Henry walked into the dressing room for a game. Ted Gavin wasn't there. Delvecchio wasn't there. Henry figured that Delvecchio was replacing Gavin and he was right. Delvecchio, although a sterling player, was not a good coach. He didn't work players hard and was from the old school and didn't use any of the newer coaching methods. The veterans were happy with him but the team slid downhill even more. The players knew they wouldn't make playoffs. There was no spark and it was very discouraging to Henry who was just trying to do his job and do it well. The '73-'74 season was a long, long season for the players.

Henry took two classes at the University of Detroit: Business Law and Micro-Economics. He liked the classes.

After the season was over it was good. Henry felt he would be staying and the team would be rebuilt and that the next year things would be different. Some of the players and Henry took a motor home to Florida and had a nice getaway.

After the southern trip, Henry went home to Warroad for a visit with his family. He was allowed to see Tara briefly. Debby was using her as a pawn to hurt Henry and his parents. His mom and dad were always proud and happy to see him and grateful that he would take time to come home. His father was working at Christian Brothers hockey stick company for $5.00 an hour. Henry helped them financially, but not as much as he wanted to, and his heart ached that he didn't have more money. He so much wanted to buy them a pretty, substantial house to replace the little clapboard near-shanty on the edge of town, and make life easier for Alice, but because Debby had wiped him out, he couldn't afford to buy them one yet.

Henry went back to Detroit for his popular hockey school that included Mites, Peewees and Bantams. He would go on the ice at 8:00 a.m. and stay there until 6:00 p.m. He was enthusiastic about his school and gave it his all.

Detroit was a mecca for Henry. He liked the fans, the people he roomed with and the people he met there. His choice would have been to have stayed and been a Red Wing for a long time but, as fate would have it, the last day of the Boucha Hockey School, Delvecchio traded Henry to the Minnesota North Stars in exchange for Danny Grant.

PART VI

STAR OF THE NORTH

GIWEDIN ANANG... "NORTH STAR"
OJIBWAY

30

Star of the North

Henry came home to the green and gold Minnesota North Stars. It was a feel-good feeling for the fans who had followed his career, and who welcomed him back as a hero. It was exciting for the other North Stars players, and the front office, who warmly received him into the fold. Henry, they knew, would attract even more fans to the already popular team.

Henry first moved in with his brother, David, and then found an apartment in Burnsville to settle into. As a seasoned player from the Junior A Jets, three years of National play, and two full seasons in the pros, he was in a great position to make his mark on the pro hockey records. It would be his third full year in the NHL.

The team played its games at the gleaming, state-of-the-art, and beloved by the fans, Met Center, where Henry had been the biggest sensation ever at the Minnesota High School State Hockey Tournament. It was there, in the game of games, where Jim Knutson's famous hit, and Henry's injury, had become part of Minnesota folklore. Henry fit into the team quickly. He always had a knack for being "one of the boys," was humble, and had a great personality that drew people to him. At that time, things were not going well for the team. Jack Gordon, North Stars' coach of ten years, said, "the team was having problems."

Randi

Henry had no sooner parked himself in Minnesota's Twin Cities when Dennis Hextall's wife, Becky, set him up on a blind date with her stunningly gorgeous friend, Randi Peterson. Randi was in nursing school at the time. The date was set to follow a North Stars game. Randi went with Becky and sat with the North Stars wives. There was a lot of excitement at the arena. The crowd was a lively group who had great pride in their North Stars. Just like his Warroad High Schools days, they couldn't get enough of Henry.

Randi watched from inside the audience as this tall, curious man with his headband and flowing thick black hair took control of the ice and everyone on it. She was aware of the charisma he generated to the fans, who were mesmerized by him. Randi had never been to a hockey game before, but it was clear to her that Henry was a wonderful skater. She became enchanted by him right along with the other fans: he was just fascinating to watch. Henry scored two goals in the game.

Afterwards Randi waited for Henry in the *wives' room* as the other players picked up their wives. Henry didn't come out for a long time. Randi was nervous. Finally he came out, dressed in a hand-tailored suit he had made for him in Montreal. The beautiful suit fit him perfectly. Henry smiled as they walked toward each other. He lifted her hand and kissed the top of it, like something out of the movies. It was clear to Randi that this beautiful man, who had a kind smile and a gentleness that transcended his strength, was the person she was about to fall in love with.

The date was going to a rib restaurant with seven other North Stars and their wives. But first Randi learned more of Henry's business than his brilliant ice performance. As they left the rink, autograph seekers at the door bombarded the couple. Randi watched as Henry patiently signed every article that every person wanted signed. In the days and months that followed, Randi also learned that every time they went to a restaurant, Henry was recognized and asked to sign napkins or whatever people had handy. He was always gracious and accommodating to everyone. This was genuine, Henry truly liked people as he had since his childhood on Buffalo Bay; that included his family and all the relatives and friends that came to visit, staying late into the night for camaraderie and warm chatter with Alice and George.

From the time they met, Henry and Randi became a couple, and life changed for Randi, who was a serious nursing student quite bogged down with studying, the classroom and hospital life. Henry's life also changed. He was happy to have a solid relationship. Randi was a very special person in her own right and was truly beautiful inside and out. Henry had dated the last year he was a Red Wing, but it was Randi who knocked his socks off. He had never been deeply in love and it was time for him to have that much-needed alliance and companionship.

Life was also fun for Randi and Henry. His ordeal with Debby was over. He was free of her debts and demands. His life was finally on track with Randi and this remarkable group of North Star players. Life for the North Stars was strenuous on the ice and the flack they took when they lost games. Fortunately, they didn't allow that to smother their ability to put it together off the ice. There was a lot of partying, eating, sharing, togetherness, and good times off-ice. People were there for each other. The players took turns having the team over. It would be a gathering at North Stars' Captain Bill Goldsworthy's (of the little dance step fondly dubbed the Goldy Shuffle) or then Lou Nanne's or the Reeds...and on and on. Randi always was included when the wives got together. It was a group of good spirits, babies, little kids, eating out, parties, and fun and Henry and Randi joined in the happy, on-going festivities with enthusiasm.

North Stars

The North Stars included the well-liked and respected 6'3", cracker-thin goalie, Cesare Maniago, who had been with the North Stars for nine years. He was an easy-going guy, always a gentleman, always polite, and he never had a bad thing to say about anybody. Maniago had followed Henry and his meteoric career with great interest since Henry had been in high school and felt Henry was the top player and going places. Maniago was happy that Henry was with the North Stars now.

Quiet, stable, older player (he was thirty-seven), Murray Oliver was one of the players everyone liked and trusted. He was a ballast for the team.

Tom Reed was a wonderful man who was a great conversation maker...and always upbeat.

Lou Nanne had a lot of interests outside of hockey and had his fingers in many areas. He was sort of a wheeler-dealer. He had lots of speaking engagements, which was good for the North Stars image. Lou was always popular with the fans.

Chippy Dennis Hextall, who lived and died by the sword, was another fan favorite. He was a very serious, responsible player. Some of the guys were yaa-hoos and out for fun, but Dennis was a fine, conscientious man on and off the ice. The thing about Dennis was that he expected everyone to give two hundred percent all the time. When the other players didn't sacrifice everything they had on the ice, it irritated him. He let them know, and very directly, how he felt about anyone who slacked.

J.P. Parise, a fan turn-on, was excellent in the corners for a little guy. Jude Drouin was loose...a good center iceman who loved to party it up, go boating and play golf. They were both good friends of Henry's on the hockey team.

Blake Dunlop, high draft choice of the North Stars from Ottawa, was Henry's best friend. They had apartments next to each other. As both were single, they hung out together on the road and at home.

Henry was tough but he was not considered a dirty player. He had so much strength, but his gentle side was apparent in his smile and his laugh that put people at ease.

the other side of the coin

Like siblings who look adorable under the tree for Christmas morning pictures, but are spatting over presents before the day is over, the North Stars did not always get along together.

When the team was playing the Boston Bruins in Boston Garden, there was an incident among the players in the locker room between periods. J.P. Parise was playing left wing on Hextall and Goldy's line. Hextall would never pass the puck to Parise. J.P. would just be skating up and down the ice waiting for the pass he never got. This went on for weeks. The only time Parise was getting to touch the puck was if he had to go after one Goldy had sent to the corner...then J.P. would have to pass it to Hextall. That made him even madder. Hextall didn't respect Parise because he wouldn't fight. It was an ongoing thing. It was between periods of the Bruins game that Parise finally blew. He clacked up to Hextall with his skates on. Hextall was a head taller, but Parise gave it all he had and jumped up quick as an Egyptian viper and punched Hextall full in the forehead. It was just a spark that ignited the rest of the team. Some others jumped in. The players who did little jousting on the ice against other teams, were fighting each other in the locker room between periods.

Goldy was well-liked, but unable to stop the bickering that sometimes broke out between the team members...usually a direct result of Hextall ragging on someone he felt was slacking.

The team was in Pittsburgh for a game and staying at a hotel. Usually the Press stayed on a different floor from the team, but a convention was in progress and rooms were tight, so the team was put on the same floor as the Press. As it happened, an initiation was going on for Peter LoPresti, a goalie from the iron range. A lot of players had been drinking. Dennis Hextall had come back from a bar and was pretty tanked. He started ragging on Parise and Drouin, whom, he felt, had not carried their weight in the game that night. It started out with words and pushing and shoving which quickly escalated into a brawl among the North Star players. The ruckus drew people who were staying at the hotel out into the hall -- or peeking around doors -- as they stared at this display wide-eyed. The Press were part of these onlookers and whisked out their ever-ready notebooks. Their pens were flying.

Goldy felt he was personally responsible for the players'

actions and for keeping harmony on the team, and that this would make him look bad. In trying to stop the melee, Goldy hit a fire extinguisher and broke his hand on the glass; he couldn't play for a month. Four of the players, including Cesare Maniago, were asleep down the hall and didn't hear about the ruckus until morning.

The press had a heyday writing up the incident between the North Stars.

the electric Indian

For Henry, the first part of the season was one of power-plays, penalty-kills and goals. True to his high school days, he set the teeth of the crowd on edge as he had in the past. He was dubbed, fondly, The Electric Indian. His colorful and exciting moves, unparalled skating, speed and shooting *were* electrifying. North Star fans, who attended those games, get a faraway look in their eye and animatedly talk about Henry as they look into their mind's telescope of that period as if it were yesterday. Teammate Murray "Muzz" Oliver, a Canadian who had been traded to the North Stars from the Maple Leafs, says that to this day he never saw anyone who could spin like Henry could. By Christmas Henry had fifteen goals and fifteen assists. Henry was built thickly by this point and was strong as a bow. There was no longer any semblance to the gangly high school kid he was identified with five years earlier. He had grown into a fabulous physique and worked to keep it that way. He would run with a full wetsuit on, to get a good sweat (two to three miles) and Randi would follow in the car. Running up and down the steps of the imposing St. Paul Cathedral, Rocky-style (before Rocky!) was another self-afflicted torture to keep fit. Randi waited on the steps when she went with him. Randi helped Henry do back exercises by lying across his feet.

Randi and Henry were becoming inseparable. Randi would take Henry to the airport and always be there to pick him up after the out-of-town games. She always enjoyed the stories when he got back.

Henry proposed to the twenty-one-year-old Randi just before Christmas, and they celebrated at a New Year's party at Lou Nanne's. They planned to be married in a gala ceremony in May.

Henry and Randi were on top of the world.

31

Goons

Back in the '50's and '60's was the start to the darker side of hockey: goons. Hockey had one or two rough guys on each team, such as John Fergeson, a Montreal Canadians winger; Reggie Fleming of the Chicago Blackhawks; Randy Holt of Los Angeles; Steve Durbano, of St. Louis; and Howie Young of Detroit. They were used for protection of their highly skilled teammates.

But by the early 1970's there were two NHL teams who really dished out rough hockey, and a new "game" showed its face. It was called "winning with intimidation." In 1970, the Boston Bruins were on top of this crash-bang game.

This type of play escalated in the next few years. The result was often brawls. In an effort to stop that kind of play the league instituted the "third man" rule. Any player who jumped in a fight between two players would also be ejected from the game along with the two primary offenders.

In the 1973-'74 season, the Flyers took this type of play another step further. The Philadelpia "Broad Street Bullies," which included "the mean ones": Dave "The Hammer" Schultz (who set a new penalty record for 348 mintues), Andre Dupont and Don Saleski, who terrorized the ice. That year the Philadelphia team tallied up 1,750 penalty minutes...an astronomical amount. Even their super-scoring captain, Bobby Clarke, was a chippy little guy. They could afford the penalties because their phenomenal goalie, Bernie Parent, kept them in the game. Philadelphia was the first team to win a Stanley Cup through thuggery. Their coach, Fearless Freddy Shero, said things like: "Get there in a hurry and be in an ugly frame of mind," and "If you keep the opposition on their behinds, they don't score goals," and, "In pro sports, the strong survive and the weak fall by the wayside." They were a brutally rough and dirty team and they won the Stanley Cup in 1974.

The other team, who was trying to catch up to the Philadelphia reputation that had usurped them, was the Boston Bruins, led by fiercely competitive Don Cherry (Rock 'em, Sock 'em Hockey) and his "bad boys," Wayne Cashman, Dave Forbes, Terry O'Reilly, Ken Hodge and "Wild Bill" McKenzie. The whole team was big and intimidating. Phil Esposito and Bobby Orr didn't back down either, nor did they need help from the other guys; they were big enough to handle themselves. Boston fans felt the surge of a powerful team, who could one-up Philadelphia. Bumper stickers, "Jesus saves and Esposito scores on the rebound," popped up on car bumpers in Boston. The Lady Byng award is awarded each year to the NHL player who exhibits sportsmanship and accomplishment. In the 1970's a sign hanging in the Boston Garden read: BEWARE, LADY BYNG DIED HERE.

***

When Boston won the Stanley Cup in 1972, Wayne Cashman, the right wing patrol for the Bruins, was partying a bit too enthusiastically. He was hauled off to jail, where he was allowed one phone call. He used it to call a Chinese restaurant to order food for himself and the other inmates.

***

When Henry was playing with the North Stars in '74-'75, it was in the middle of the thug era. The North Stars did not have a reputation as being a nasty team...in fact they were criticized for not having enough spine and for backing down to the goon teams. Aside from rugged Dennis Hextall, who always had his guard up and who wouldn't take any "guff" from anybody, the team was actually quite mild. Hextall was intense; not a vicious player, but he stood up to the rough guys on the other teams and wanted the help of the other players in doing the same. Dennis O'Brien and Bill Goldworthy scrapped, and didn't seem to mind it, and Fred Barrett made his name as a hard hitter. Henry was not a goon, but was intimidating to the opposition by sheer size and strength. He *would* fight, but because of his skills he was not primarily a fighter.

***

Finesse players over the years have battled for clean play and, as a result, hockey is getting away from the fighting and needless rough play. Fighting takes away a lot from the superstar. The automatic *third man in* ejection rule that had been instituted way back in 1971, didn't just mean just fighting, it could mean just jawing at each other. In recent years Wayne Gretzky and Mario Lemieux have led the campaign against the thug-type hockey. In order to clean up the sport they have spoken out vehemently against violence. Currently hockey has a new face and has evolved more toward the "clutch and grab" game, but the fans are still hungry for the style Henry had – the player that could wow them by skills.

Akando: "ambush"

The date of the most vicious assault in sports history was January 4th, 1975. Henry, the kind people-person who was always there for the fans and ready with a sincere and warm smile; the player who had worked for almost twenty years to perfect his skating and his skills, was twenty-four years old. The light was burning bright within him; the Ojibway drums of his soul were beating in Henry harmoniously.

***

The North Stars were playing the Boston Bruins in the Met Center that evening. Bob Utecht, announcer and sports writer, recalled that in the morning the North Stars had a press meeting headed up by Gordy Ritz, president of the North Stars. (Utecht had recently written an article concerning the Bruins' profanity that was being targeted at the minor officials: the timekeepers and scorekeepers, and also to the announcers.) The Press was concerned about the actions of the Bruins and how the North Star's would handle it. There was pressure on the North Stars' players to be more aggressive towards the bullies. The fans were very interested in this game. That evening the Met Center housed the largest crowd of the season...and what they would see would be ugly.

the game

Henry was playing on the first line with center Dennis Hextall and Muzz Oliver on the other wing. Don Cherry, premier advocate for violence in hockey, then coach of the Boston Bruins, put out his third Bruins forward checking line (defensive line) of borderline NHL players (the enforcement) against them. This line included Dave Forbes and Terry O'Reilly. These were the goons who would shadow the good players and try to take them off the game, breaking their concentration by hooking, slashing, elbowing, etc. (Bobby Orr, the Bruins' impact-defenseman, was also on the ice.) It was clear to the North Stars' players, coaches and fans what the Bruins intended. It was time for the goons to intimidate the North Stars.

Dave Forbes had been agitating Henry the entire game. Henry

went to his zone to pick up the puck. It had been dumped in his defensive corner. Dave Forbes took a vicious run at Henry, elbows high, from the top of the circle. Henry, who was carrying the puck, saw him from the corner of his eye. He dead-stopped to slip Forbes...Forbes sailed past Henry and smashed into the glass. Fists flew as Henry and Forbes fought. Henry got the best of the fight but, when they went down in a pile, Bruins' goon, Terry O'Reilly, jumped on Henry's back. The referee called coincidental penalties on Henry and Forbes. They both went to the penalty box for two minutes for roughing and a five-minute fighting penalty. O'Reilly was kicked out of the game.

Forbes was quickly followed to the box by Bobby Orr. Orr was sent in to serve a five-minute major for slashing Hextall's face with his stick and cutting his cheek. It took four stitches to fix Hextall up. (Later in the game Orr got a misconduct penalty for throwing a tantrum in the penalty box.) Henry was alone in his box. There were words flying over the glass between Orr, Forbes and Henry, and threats from Forbes to Henry about "getting" him. To quote the *Minneapolis Star* "Forbes held up a clenched fist and shouted across to Boucha, 'I'll get you and I won't use this, I'll shove my stick down your throat'." (Henry didn't hear the threat because of the crowd noise.)

Play stopped. It was time for Henry and Forbes to get out of the box. Henry briefly glanced at Forbes, who looked like things had settled down and that he wouldn't try anything else at the time. Then, as he skated out from the box dragging his stick, Henry checked his bench to see if he was supposed to stay on the ice and play or go back to the bench. In that split second Henry heard a fan shout "Look Out!" He turned just in time to see the blunt end of Forbes stick inches in front of his eye.

To the utter horror of everyone in attendance that night in the Met Center, Dave Forbes was using his stick as a warrior or demented person would use a spear, bayonet or rifle butt -- and it was aimed smack at Henry's face. There was no mistake about it. It was a cold, calculated move that gave the fans and players alike a sick feeling, and that everyone interviewed almost twenty-five years later never forgot. Dave Forbes was a very strong man. He attacked from behind. Henry, the boy who had worked so hard to become the best, who had done it alone, and who had spent his life perfecting his skating and his skills, had no warning. The force was brutal.

All the pain in the universe cracked through Henry's body as the stick attached to Forbes' rage attacked his eye. He felt the bone shatter. He felt his eye pushed in as he fell to the ice with blood from his eye spurting onto the ice. An attack by the feared Viet Cong couldn't have been more painful. The stunned crowd screamed in fury. Henry did not fight back: he was unconscious to semi-conscious. He sunk to the ice with the blood spurting from his eye. His hands intuitively covered his face. It was clear the hero was hurt badly. Then, in an unparalleled episode of American sports history, Forbes jumped on Henry's back and continued punching him, beating him, beating him, punching him and banging Henry's lifeless looking head on the ice as Henry's body tried to crawl away. All the time the blood was spilling and flying, leaving the ice looking like the finger-painting of a mad man. John Gilbert wrote, in the *Minneapolis Star*, Sunday January 5th, 1975, "Forbes jumped on top of Boucha, who was sprawled face down in a widening pool of blood and continued punching in the most savage assault Met Center officials said they had ever witnessed."

Murray Oliver, who saw this barbarous attack out of the corner of his eye, raced over to pull Forbes off Henry. He knew this was serious and could see the officials were doing nothing; obviously Henry couldn't fight back. Cesare Maniago left his crease to help his fallen friend. Oliver, who prevented Henry from getting hurt any worse than he was, and perhaps from being killed, was ejected from the game and Cesare Maniago received a penalty for leaving the crease.

As his teammates gathered around Henry's limp body, a policeman entered the penalty box with Forbes, who was casually wiping the sweat off his forehead as if he had just run the four-minute mile. Henry was loaded onto a sterile white stretcher, to the silence of the crowd, who was feeling a white-raging hostility toward the Boston Bruins, and this wild frenzy of destruction to their own Minnesota favorite son. Henry's buddies flanked the stretcher like pallbearers -- heads bowed, helmets off -- as they skated beside Henry on the stretcher, for the long, slow trip across the ice. Bill Goldsworthy, who was not playing because of his injured hand, went quietly to get a dazed Randi out of the crowd and take her to where Henry was.

The finesse *player of players*, the most beautiful skater to play the game, had been felled by a goon. As the light went out on his hockey-world, the dirge of the Ojibway drums, the barometer of his soul, thumped dolefully within him. His mind hadn't comprehended what had happened yet, but his body knew his blazing career, and the dreams that went with it, was ended.

EPILOGUE

justice according to Campbell

The question on everyone's mind was what would happen to Dave Forbes. Clarence Campbell, the commissioner of the NHL, came to town and interviewed fans and players. He wrote down everything in laborious longhand. Then he made his decision, which stunned Henry and the Minnesota hockey world. Campbell handed down a mere ten-game suspension without pay to Forbes, which translated to a three week time period. A mere slap on the wrist. Three weeks for ending Henry's career. At a time when Campbell could have made a statement and stopped the goon side of hockey, he didn't. Instead of protecting the players, he chose to protect the game.

Hennepin County trial

The Hennepin County officials, disgusted at the NHL decision, decided to bring suit against Forbes and wanted Henry to be a witness. If the league wouldn't control the violence, they reasoned, the county would. The county attorneys felt (and rightly so) that if this malicious attack had been done on the street the person would be in jail. The lawyers interviewed eyewitnesses and Henry. This was the first time in the history of U.S. professional sports of any incident from the playing field being brought to court. Gary Flackne was the head lawyer in the case and Ron Meshbesher was Forbes' attorney. Violence in hockey was the theme.

Henry was not a good witness. He felt intimidated by the NHL and, of course, was hoping a miracle would restore his eye and that he would be able to play pro hockey again. He didn't want to jeopardize his chances to return. (Henry was seeing double, and though he has had repeated surgeries, he still sees double.) Bob Utecht was a good witness. He volunteered to testify without a subpoena, did not mince words, did not buckle under the pounding he took on the stand, and told it like it was. To show how the trial went: Don Wheeler, who was a former catcher for the White Sox, was the penalty timekeeper. He was fifteen feet from Henry when the attack occurred. Front and center he saw Forbes go after and ram Henry, but because Henry was faced the other direction and Wheeler didn't actually see the stick hit the eye, his testimony was considered irrelevant!

The trial resulted in a hung jury because one man liked violence in hockey.

Later that summer, Henry and Utecht were not invited to the

Duff's Golf Classic, a golf outing attended by hockey personalities. Forbes was invited! Forbes, charged with a vicious assult 15,000 people saw committed, was a celebrity at the charity golf tournament...a big slam to Henry.

Henry's civil trial

Henry brought civil action against the Boston Bruins, Dave Forbes and the NHL. The Boston Bruins, because Don Cherry had told Forbes to go after Henry; Dave Forbes, for his actions; and the NHL for negligence. The case, with its interrogatories and depositions, went on for five years. The day before the case was scheduled to go to court the four parties involved met. It looked like a lawyer's convention with all the attorneys for all the sides present. Henry received a separate amount of money from each entity. There is a gag order on this and to this day Henry cannot talk about his settlement in dollars. He is grateful for something but it was not enough for the loss of his eye and his career. He feels that if the case had gone to court he would have fared better.

the end

Henry and Randi were married, but not in the grand wedding they had planned. The simple ceremony in May of 1975 included only family. The dashing groom, who didn't know then that he would see double for the rest of his life, had a large bandage over his eye and was facing surgery in Rochester's Mayo Clinic the following week. Randi and Henry had two children. The marriage, sadly, ended in separation eight years later. Henry was not able to cope with the loss of his dream and what he had worked so many years to achieve.

In one heinous act, Dave Forbes took Henry's eyesight, his life's dream, his identity, his spirit that had burned so brightly, and his marriage.

the question

The question remains. "What could Henry have accomplished had his vision not been robbed from him?"

To this day, the soul of the boy who so elegantly skated himself into the hearts of thousands is haunted by that question.

ACKNOWLEDGEMENTS

Thank you David Boucha, for your sharp memories of Buffalo Bay, family history and Warroad of the 1950's, which enabled me to write the early chapters.

Thank you to Darlene Boucha Dorion, Shirley Boucha Flick, and Jim Boucha for filling in family history, and to Irene Boucha Bobcyzinski for providing old family photographs.

Thank you Tara, Henry Jr., Bridgette, and J.P., Henry Boucha's *great kids,* for politeness – always, when Andy and I visited Warroad, and to Elaine for her wonderful hospitality.

Thank you to Ruth Stukel and Beth Marvin for opening up the Warroad Library Heritage Center to Henry's archives.

Thank you Myron Grafstrom and John Hopkins, coaches with early impact on Henry's career, and Dick Roberts and Dale Telle, who coached his later high school years...for sharing memories. Thank you Frank Krahn and Lyle Kvarnlov: Henry's "Warrior" teammates, for their high school perceptions of Henry. An added thank you to Frank for the radio tapes of Bernie Bergraff announcing the 1969 Championship game and to Lyle for loaning me his Warroad Warriors scrapbook. Thank you to Roseau Rams, Earl Anderson and Dale Smedsmo and Edina's Bruce Carlson, who gave me a view of the opposition.

Thank you to the 1970 and 1971 National Team and 1972 Olympic coach, icon Murray Williamson, for the time and insight into three years of Henry's life that formed him into the stuff that NHLers are made of, and for writing the foreword to this book. Thank you to Dr. George Nagobads for his time, stories and pictures. Thank you to Kathy and Frank Sanders, Tana and Mike Curran, Evie and "Huffer" Christianson, Dick McGlynn, Wally Olds, Bruce McIntosh, Pete Sears, and Stu Irving, for player insights into the National and Olympic teams and for old clippings and pictures.

Thank you to Cesare Maniago, Murray Oliver and Jack Gordon for talking to me about the North Stars era.

Thank you to Bob Utecht, writer and announcer, for sharing his memories of the "Forbes incident" and the trial.

Thank you to Marvin Windows and Doors for opening up their flights and saving Henry and me the long drives from Minnetonka to Warroad for interviews, picture searching and re-reads.

Thank you to the *Minneapolis Star Tribune* Librarian, Robert Jansen; Craig Campbell, historian, *Hockey Hall of Fame;* Marilyn Rader, *AP World Wide Photos;* and Julie Hill, *Corbis Images.* Thank you to *Let's Play Hockey's* Doug Johnson and Shane Frederick for being there with information when we needed it.

Thank you to Glenda Gausen for the nights at The Good Earth proofreading with me to make a cleaner copy for the editors.

Thank you to my friend, Judy Gessner Callas, for believing in my writing and listening to the woes of it all, along with the triumphs.

Thank you Christine May, for coming to the rescue in the eleventh hour and creating the cover design.

Thank you to Glen Carlson for his incredible knowledge of hockey history, his descriptions of Henry Boucha, the star, and the skater that he so eloquently described to me, and for reading the manuscript, and offering valuable suggestions for making the book a fuller, richer piece.

Thank you to my father, Herbert G. Halverson, for passing on to me an appreciation of literature, love of this unique state of Minnesota, and especially for making sure I had a background, caring and understanding of the plight of the indigenous peoples.

Thank you to Colleen Wasner and David Starke for absolute brilliance in editing, which also includes long and arduous hours of very hard work.

Thank you to my husband, Darrell, for putting up with what spouses of writers have to endure. And thank you to my son, Andy, for your humor when I needed it and your levelness when I needed that.

Thank you to Randi Boucha, for letting me into her heart and her memories.

And most of all thank you, Henry, for transcending the ordinary and giving us a star.

HENRY BOUCHA: STAR OF THE NORTH
...biography of a superstar

$14.95 U.S. (Minnesota residents add $1.04 tax per book ordered)
plus $1.50 mailing and add $.50 per additional book.

and

RIVER OF CHAMPIONS
A hockey story

...a tribute to a group of common Minnesota teenage boys, whose single goal (and path to reach it) turned them into extraordinary young men. The fast paced, tightly written story traces their passion, desire, trials, failures and ultimate triumph, as it plays out against the stark background of a frigid winter in a far-north Minnesota town. In a story of twists and surprises, the boys transform the little town into a collective of hold-your-breath excitement and pride.
The story is a treatise of never giving up,
and of what man can be when he believes in himself and others.

$11.95 U.S. (Minnesota residents add $.68 tax per book ordered)
plus $1.50 mailing and add $.50 per additional book.

may be ordered from

SNOWSHOE PRESS   P.O. Box 24334   Edina, MN 55345
612-975-0838

Amount enclosed _____

Number of copies: Star of the North _____

Number of copies: River of Champions _____

Name _____

Street or Box _____

City, State, Zip _____

Phone number _____

Thank you for your order